THE SUPERSTONE®
COUNTRY KITCHEN
STONEWARE COOKBOOK

By Kay Emel-Powell

Illustrated by Mary Parks
Cover Illustration by Allen Eisbrener

sassafras press
P. O. Box 1366
Evanston, Illinois 60204

LIBRARY OF CONGRESS CATALOG CARD NUMBER: 82-061859
ISBN NUMBER: 0-930528-05-0

First Printing First Edition   September, 1982
Second Printing   December, 1983
Third Printing   May, 1992

INTRODUCTION

Clay cookery is becoming increasingly popular in this country. Americans are finding that the even heating and moisture absorption properties of Stoneware produce a better baked and more nutritiously cooked meal.

Clay cooking is, however, the oldest organized method of preparing food. The Egyptians baked on rocks in the sun and the early Athenians carried a portable brick oven with them as they traveled.

The Superstone® Country Kitchen Stoneware Cookbook combines mouthwatering recipes with practical tips for how to prepare honest-to-goodness "Down-home" meals in, on and under stoneware.

Mary Parks, a freelance artist and teacher, who so delightfully illustrated the book, lives in Batavia, Illinois, with her husband, Stan, and their son, Brad.

Kay Emel-Powell, was raised with "country kitchen" cooking and her recipes demonstrate her unique ability to communicate this classic form of American cooking. Kay lives in Minneapolis, Minnesota with her husband, Mark, and is currently writing another cookbook.

Steven Schwab
Publisher

ACKNOWLEDGEMENTS

A cookbook is rarely just one person's doing. This project, completed over eleven months, had its basis in years of baking and years of thinking and learning about American country food. And so, for all those friends and relatives who kept asking, "Are you working on a cookbook yet?" and to Steven Schwab and Nancy Polakow, who asked me to write this book for Sassafras Enterprises, I offer heartfelt thanks.

Gourmet retailers in the Upper Midwest, for whom I represented Sassafras, are enthusiastic about Superstone® products. They shared the enthusiasm with me, along with many ideas and experiences. They are an inspiration to me.

Inspiration also came from a number of food writers. Looking at shelves filled with cookbooks, I realize my first was Margaret Rudkin's **The Pepperidge Farm Cookbook.** I won this when I was about 16 as part of the prize for being the county 4-H baking champion. Its pages provided much of my initial inspirations.

Being one who enjoys reading about the history of food, it's little wonder that books by James Beard and Elizabeth David are fairly numerous on my shelves as well.

No list of inspiring American food writers would be complete without mention of Clementine Paddleford. Her food columns were part of our Sunday paper when I was growing up. Knowing she was also from Kansas has always been a source of pride for me.

There are nameless bakers in bakeries from one corner of this country to the other who also have added to my experience. Some special people have shared these travels, but a favorite companion, my husband Mark Powell, deserves the most credit. He always lets me stop.

Mark deserves credit for his help with this book in countless other ways too — from hours of helping to proof and edit manuscripts to a willingness to sample just about every recipe.

Most of all, however, this book is lovingly dedicated to Clara Emel, my mother, for whom "homemade" is a way of life.

KAY EMEL-POWELL
Minneapolis
August 1982

TABLE OF CONTENTS

Page

I. Superstone® Baking Stones and
Superstone® Baking Tiles 13

II. French Bread Baker 45

III. Baking Crocks 51

IV. La Cloche 65

V. Deep Dish Pizza and Pie Baker 79

VI. Index 97

THE SUPERSTONE®
COUNTRY KITCHEN
STONEWARE COOKBOOK

INTRODUCTION
SOME NOTES ON BAKING

There was a time when if you thought about a baking pan, you'd have only thought about a metal one. Little else was available. Recently, however, people have begun finding a pleasure in baking with what is probably the oldest form of cookware: clay. With the various Superstone products used in this book, you'll not only bake **in** clay, but **on** clay and **under** clay.

Clay wares are distinguished by how they are fired and glazed. Superstones are natural stoneware. Fired at temperatures over 2000°, the clay becomes nearly vitrified -- meaning that the clay becomes glasslike. The term natural is used because Superstones are made from a single un-refined clay and are unglazed, factors which contribute to its greater absorption of heat and moisture.

The Superstone came into being because Sassafras Enterprises was looking for a way the home baker and pizza maker could duplicate the quality of crustiness which professionals get from baking in brick ovens. What was good for pizza made sense for yeast breads and other baked goods too.

Baking tiles, the baking crocks, and the deep dish pizza/pie baker were created, followed a little later by the French bread baker and the individual quiche dishes.

In times when more people than ever are baking, and are more concerned with the quality of what they bake, Superstones have become a prime choice for baking. Because the unglazed stoneware absorbs heat readily, and retains that heat, an oven's heat is diffused evenly while the food is baking. Yeast breads achieve desired crustiness. Rich heavy cakes bake almost as if steamed. Hearty deep dish pies heat to bubbly goodness before crusts have a chance to burn.

But what of the idea of baking "under" clay? People who study food have suspected for years that it's not just the brick of the oven which contributes to the final glory of a country loaf of bread. The fact that the oven was sealed and the heat slackened during the baking were also factors. Elizabeth David, the marvelous English food writer, experimented with several systems to achieve the steamy atmosphere of the country cottage's brick oven. From her work came the idea of baking under a pottery bowl.

But a pottery bowl large enough to accomodate a rising loaf is cumbersome. The quality of the unglazed Superstone was already recognized for baking bread. Designing a half-sphere Superstone piece with a handle to accompany a pottery base was a logical next step. The French call this shape a **cloche;** Sassafras calls its baker La Cloche.

People who have baked bread for years are utterly astounded at the results. It's as if we'd stopped believing four simple ingredients -- flour, yeast, water, and salt -- could rise to such heights, and be such a vision of golden crustiness and fully developed crumb. Eating breads from La Cloche, spread with sweet cream butter, is a bread lover's delight.

La Cloche can also be used as a clay cooker for the long slow cooking that characterizes pot roasting or braising.

From these concepts of baking materials and baking methods came the idea for a country baking book. Be it top-knotted Pumpkin Loaf, peppery south of the border pizza, or an Orange Baked Chicken, recipes were chosen for their hearty country goodness.

Good cooks always remember their first kitchens. Ours was a country kitchen where baking was accomplished with fresh ingredients and simplicity. It took me years to realize that not everyone grew up on "homebaked" breads, cookies, and pies. Becoming a baker, and now a Superstone baker, was a course started early in life. In subtle ways the knowledge was imparted from mother to daughter.

Even if baking is not in your family tradition, there are many ways to learn baking now. Cooking classes, wonderful cookbooks, or inspiration from a visit to a gourmet kitchenware store may be all the encouragements you need. The aromas that baking brings to your home, and the pleasure that comes from doing it, are special rewards.

Some of my food biases will be evident in this book. Even if we're busy people, it makes sense to me that if we take time for home baking we should use the best ingredients we can.

One of my first projects when I move to new places is to find a meat market, a grocer or a farmer who has a sense of fresh food, and a source for "from scratch" baking staples.

A kitchen garden where tomatoes, zucchini, salad greens, green beans, and a variety of herbs can be grown is also high on my personal list of needs.

When first using these recipes, it may seem that all the mixing is done by hand. That's not the case. A food processor and a heavy-duty mixer with a dough hook are constant allies of mine. Recipes have been written to follow the generally suggested procedures for these two kitchen helpers. Kneading breads and pizza dough, at least in part, is, however, always accomplished by hand. There is a "rightness" to the feel of properly kneaded yeast dough that can only come from getting your hands into it.

Before long you'll find your own favorite pieces of stoneware and recipes that seem your own, made from ingredients that may vary with the time of year or where you've shopped that day. Baking is a little more precise than some cooking because of the interplay of specific ingredients and the chemical reactions that take place. But there is still lots of room for creativity, and once mastered baking is never something that takes too much time.

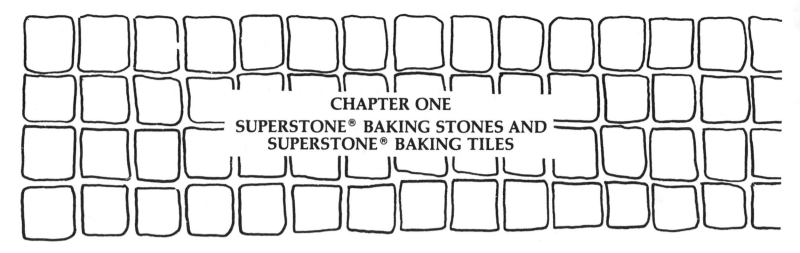

CHAPTER ONE
SUPERSTONE® BAKING STONES AND
SUPERSTONE® BAKING TILES

Superstone baking tiles may be used in several ways. The most traditional way is to put them on your oven rack to preheat with the oven. Whatever you are baking is assembled on a baking peel. The peel, a wooden board with finely tapered edges, is then used to slide your creation into and out of the oven.

While this method works well for pizza and firm whole grain loaves, using metal baking pans or cookie sheets is an easier way to bake with the tiles. The effect of using the tiles remains the same. A few minutes before the baking is finished, remove bread loaves from the pans, and let the loaves finish browning directly on the tile surface.

The Superstone baking stone can be used in place of a cookie sheet. Simply shape a yeast bread or pizza on the Superstone baking stone, or use it for cookies, bread sticks, scones, and biscuits.

This chapter contains all the basics on bread baking, so if you are a novice, this is the place to start.

Since many of the recipes for breads are for two loaves, I've gotten into the practice of using half the dough for a free-form loaf, and using the remaining half for a pan loaf they are easier to slice for sandwiches and toast. Sometimes the free-form loaf is baked by the undercover method described in the La Cloche chapter; sometimes the remaining dough is divided between two baking crocks.

Breads And Yeast Baking

People start baking bread for all kinds of reasons. I grew up on the marvelous Graham Health Bread in this chapter, and have for years baked it with a regularity far exceeding any other kind. Having this bread in the house for toast with jam to start my day has always been reason enough for me to make bread. Made with a mixture of graham and all-purpose flour, sweetened with brown sugar and molasses, texture made tender with the addition of shortening and milk, this is classic "homemade" bread. While it always tastes more or less the same to me, the ingredients it contains, the methods of making it, how it's baked, and what shape it has varies with each baking.

This variety is what makes baking bread the most creative of cooking techniques. Some people start baking bread almost without knowing it when they begin making dough for pizza. One step leads naturally to another, maybe from the desire to recreate a memorable sourdough French bread or from a desire for particular holiday bread fragrant with spices and jeweled with fruit.

Ingredients For Yeast Bread Baking

The simplest loaves of bread have only four ingredients: flour, yeast, water, and salt. All other kinds of bread are variations on this simple theme.

Flour. The kind of flour used determines the nature of the bread. An all-purpose flour made from wheat contains enough of the protein called gluten to result in a loaf with good volume. Through the process of mixing and kneading, the gluten is "developed." This process gives yeast breads their fine even texture.

Most recipes contain part, if not all, all-purpose flour. In experimenting with flours for this book, I used several different brands, some from major mills and some from small specialty millers. Unbleached all-purpose flour is used in the recipes.

All-purpose flour bought in 25-pound bags is generally of higher protein content because mills expect that people who buy that quantity are bread bakers. A "hard wheat" flour, one from the winter wheat growing areas of the country, is essential for French-type breads, and is, in fact, the best for any bread. You **will** notice differences with this flour.

Because flour varies in texture and absorbancy, how it's measured for a recipe makes a difference. All the flour for this book was measured by spooning the flour lightly into a measuring cup, then leveling it off with a spatula. I use a kitchen scale to weigh out flour. Measuring as described here yields four cups of all-purpose flour to the pound. Using stone-ground whole grain flours in recipes will change this proportion, requiring less flour. Older recipes and those from other countries seem to require less flour. This is because foreign flours are not "pre-sifted" as is our all-purpose flour.

A basic loaf can change in character quite markedly when various specialty flours or other grains are used. The bran and germ of the wheat which are removed in the milling of all-purpose flour can be added back. Miller's bran and wheat germ are the basic components; whole wheat and graham flours are those milled leaving the bran and germ intact. Stone-ground versions of these flours are generally more coarsely ground, and add a nuttiness to breads that I prefer.

Cracked wheat, steel-cut oats, and a variety of whole grains used for cereals make interesting additions to bread. Health food and specialty grocers are the sources for these items. A seven-grain cereal and the Irish oatmeal are also used here, as are stone-ground cornmeal and rolled oats.

Rye flours are available in light, medium, and dark varieties; the light being milled like an all-purpose flour, the others having bran and germ included. Rye flour can be used by itself, but is usually used in combination with all-purpose flour. Triticale, a flour derived from a man-made cross between rye and wheat, gives a distinctive nutty flavor to bread that is worth trying in recipes using whole wheat flour.

Soy flour is an addition to bread made primarily to boost protein content and quality. A tablespoon or so per cup of flour can be used.

Many whole grain flours need storage in the refrigerator or in some cool part of the house. If you forget to let the flour come to room temperature before using it, the rising time of the dough will be slower. A simple remedy is to put the flour you'll use in a covered mixing bowl and put it in a very low oven (200°) for five minutes before you begin baking.

Yeast. Yeast is the leavening in breads. This remarkable microscopic plant is "activated" with warmth and sugar, and gives off carbon dioxide which causes the bread to rise.

Active dry yeasts are the most readily available and I used them for recipe testing. A preservative-free yeast available in health food stores and food co-ops has always been my personal choice. Compressed yeast, a cake-form, is also a good choice, but must be used within a fairly short time period (about two weeks).

Sourdough starters are a method of leavening yeast bread, and are discussed later in this chapter.

Amounts of yeast used vary depending on the other ingredients and the amount of time allowed for the bread to rise. As a general rule, I use a scant tablespoon or one package yeast for each four to six cups of flour used.

The "mixer method" of making bread, where yeast is not dissolved first but simply blended with dry ingredients, uses more yeast. At one point, I made nearly all my bread by this method, but I find myself using more "old-fashioned" methods these days. I like the firmer texture that comes with longer rising and the lack of "yeastiness" that lets me taste all the wonderful stone-ground grains that many of the recipes call for.

Water and other liquids. Liquid binds the flour and yeast together. The ratio of flour to water is about four to one. Water is used for the crustier breads, while milk is used for "home-style" breads.

Older recipes always say to "scald the milk," a step not necessary with milk that has been pasteurized. These same recipes sometimes call for "water in which potatoes have cooked." This is an addition which produces bread with a marvelous moist crumb.

Salt and other ingredients. Salt usage is a much discussed topic. While many people recommend leaving it out entirely, its presence in bread is needed for more than its flavor. Salt tempers the fermenting process, thus contributing to the evenness of a bread's texture.

To a certain extent the amount of salt used to flavor bread will be based on the kind of butter used to spread on it. People who use only unsalted butter will probably add more salt to the bread they make. In the same sense, this adjustment will be made if the recipe contains butter. As a rule of thumb, one tablespoon salt is generally used for each four cups, or one pound, of flour.

Butter and oils used in bread contribute to their tenderness and flavor. Again, crusty breads usually contain very little shortening, with the exception being some French-type breads flavored with olive oil. These shortening ingredients also contribute favorably to a bread's keeping quality.

Sugar or other sweetners like molasses or honey are not essential, but again, they contribute to bread's tenderness and golden color of the crust. The flavor they add to breads that are toasted is particularly pleasing.

The role of sugar to "activate" the yeast is a practice I sometimes question, but it is followed in this book. Many food authorities and some yeast manufacturers recommend that "yeast be dissolved in water with sugar and allowed to proof until foamy." Yeasts today seem to be of a fairly high quality, you need not be too concerned with "dead" yeast. However, until you've gained experience with particular brands, it's probably a good practice to activate your yeast with sugar.

Eggs are added to make a richer dough, and are usually added to sweet breads and rolls. The batter breads in the Baking Crock chapter also contain them.

Steps In Making Yeast Bread

The techniques used in making bread can seem awesome to a person just learning. Certain phrases appear in recipes that beg for explanations. Some of these phrases are described below. These steps will soon become part of your repertoire of cooking knowledge.

Dissolve yeast in warm water and sugar; let it proof. This step "activates" the dry yeast by warming and feeding it. The warm water is between about 105° F. to 115° F., or comfortably warm on your wrist when held under running water. Sprinkle the yeast into the water, add the sugar, and stir until yeast and sugar are dissolved. Set this mixture aside. After a few minutes, the proofing will have started, and the mixture will appear foamy.

Let cool to lukewarm. In recipes where whole grains or cereals are used, the liquid is heated to boiling and poured over the grains to soften them. "Lukewarm" is room temperature, or a temperature no higher than that used to dissolve the yeast.

Add part of the flour and other ingredients; blend well. The mixing step distributes the yeast among the other ingredients, and is a step many people accomplish with a mixer. This initial mixing begins the gluten development, and when done for about 3 to 5 minutes can reduce kneading time by half.

In some of the recipes there is a "sponging" step at this point. A sponge is made by mixing the yeast, liquid and sweetening ingredients with some of the flour, then allowing the mixture to stand until bubbly and increased in volume. In sweet breads this step allows the liquid to be absorbed by both the flour and sugar, and prevents too much flour from being added to the dough. In breads with stone-ground grain, it also allows time for moisture to be absorbed so only limited amounts of flour are added during kneading.

Stir in enough additional flour . . . Depending on the kind of flour, the temperature and the humidity, the dough will absorb additional flour. As the flour is stirred in, a little at a time, the dough will leave the sides of the bowl, forming a bowl. Recipes will describe either a soft or stiff dough, or a stiff batter.

Turn out on lightly floured board and knead . . . The kneading step further stretches the developing gluten, and distributes the yeast throughout the dough. Many people find kneading soothing and relaxing, and consider this the best part of baking homemade bread.

Flour is added to the kneading surface and your hands to keep them from sticking to the dough. A pastry scraper is sometimes used to fold over soft doughs a few times when the doughs are initially sticky to handle.

Begin kneading by bring the edges of the dough toward you, then push it away with the heels and your hands. Give the dough a quarter turn, and repeat, developing your own speed and rhythm.

More flour will usually be needed, but use only enough to keep the dough from sticking to the board. After a few minutes, the dough will fit the description of "smooth and elastic."

Adding too much flour is a fairly common mistake during kneading. The dough should remain soft and pliable. The kneading time depends on how the dough was mixed, the flour used, and the temperature; but in general, five to ten minutes will do. One measure of well-kneaded dough is that you see tiny blisters forming just under the surface of the dough. Another measure is to make an indentation in the dough with a finger; the hole will spring back if the dough is ready.

Place dough in greased bowl, and turn to coat surface. The bowl used should be large enough for the dough to double in size. Grease or butter the bowl, then roll the ball of dough around the bowl so that the dough is lightly coated. This step keeps the dough from drying out as it rises, as does covering the bowl with plastic wrap or a towel.

Let rise in a warm place until doubled in size. The rising step leavens the bread by allowing the yeast to grow, and in the process causes the volume of the dough to increase. At the same time, the gluten is further developing the structure that will give the bread its final texture.

In most recipes, breads rise at least once at this point, and then again after shaping. Some recipes suggest another rise which contributes to a finer finished texture. A second or third rise is always quicker than the first.

Temperature is again important at this point. The optimum "warm place" is 80° to 85° and draft-free. Find a good spot (mine's on top of the refrigerator), and let the dough rise for an hour or two. When dough has risen enough, a fingertip indentation made in the dough will remain open.

A pilotless gas or electric oven can be turned on to 400° for about a minute to achieve a warm place. Ovens with pilot lights will keep dough warm, although occasionally some are too warm. Yeast will grow at lower temperatures, even in the refrigerator, but will take much longer. This is helpful to remember as breadmaking sometimes gets interrupted.

Punch down the dough. This step is accomplished by "punching down" lightly with a fist in the center of the dough, and then gently pulling the outer edges to the center.

Bake . . . until loaves sound hollow when tapped. Like the "smooth and elastic" of kneading, this phrase is subjective. Generally, when breads are baked they also pull away from the sides of the pan, and of course, brown. You'll find having baking tiles in the oven helps breads to bake more evenly, but you may want to tap both the top and the bottom of the loaf to check for doneness. As one writer said. "you'll learn to distinguish the dull thud of an undone loaf from the hollow thump of a done one."

Remove from pans onto a rack to cool. This step is recommended for any pan, but is particularly important for Superstone pieces. Since breads cool slowly, steam softens the loaves you've worked so hard to get crusty. Breads should be completely cooled before storing for the same reason. Allow at least two to three hours for cooling.

Shaping Breads

What distinguishes the bread of one region or another is often the loaf's shape. Becoming familiar with different shapes is a study of breadmakings. Baking free-form

loaves on Superstone tiles is an opportunity to try some of these shapes, or to invent some of your own.

To shape a **basic pan loaf**, roll or pat the dough into a rectangle with the short side equal to the length of the bread pan. Roll up the dough, jelly-roll fashion.

1. Pinch the seam firmly to seal. Tuck the ends of the dough under to seal. Place the loaf in a greased loaf pan, making sure it is even at both ends.

2. To shape a **basic free-form loaf**, shape the dough by tucking the edges underneath into a tight rounded ball or oval. Place on Superstone or cookie sheet sprinkled with cornmeal.

(Before baking, slash tops deeply with a sharp knife or scissors. Brush with an egg wash for a crisper crust. Crisscross or checkerboard cuts make particularly crusty loaves).

3. Letting dough rise in a heavily floured French banneton, then turning onto tiles to bake, gives you a **classic beehive-shaped loaf**.

4. Dough may be flattened by rolling or patting into the desired size or shape.

5. A **cottage loaf** is shaped using about a third of the dough for a topknot. The loaf can be brushed with butter or sprinkled with flour before baking.

6. The **coiled loaf** uses a third of the dough for a topknot coil. Roll a strand the dough with the palms of your hands to shape a coil and place on the larger loaf, tucking ends under securely so they will not uncoil during baking. Brush with butter.

7. **French-style loaves** are shaped by rolling strands of dough between the palms of your hands and your work surface until loaves are of the desired length. Place on Superstone, French bread baker, or cookie sheet sprinkled with cornmeal.

8. **Vienna-type loaves** have one or two long "leaf-shaped" cuts. An English bloomer is cut with a number of scroll-type cuts. French and Italian breads have several diagonal cuts. Remember to brush with a glaze before baking.

9. **Twist loaves** are made by twisting two bread strands together with as many turns as possible. Tuck ends under. Two different kinds of doughs make interesting slices in the finished loaf.

10. For **braided loaves**, roll three strands of dough to desired length. Braid the strands together. To make a wreath, shape the braid into a ring. Use a small portion of dough to make a bow over the seam.

11. For **bread sticks**, shape by rolling strands of dough into pencil shapes between the palms of your hands and a well-oiled work surface. For breadstick twists, pick up the strand, holding an end in each hand, and twist, turning clockwise in one hand and counter clockwise in the other.

12. **Pretzels** are shaped like bread sticks, then given a final stretch before rolling into pretzel shapes. Tuck ends under.

Throughout this book recipes will refer to various egg washes or glazes. These are brushed on lightly just before baking. Sometimes a specific wash or glaze is suggested but they are usually interchangeable.

For French breads or crusty loaves, either a whole egg or egg white is beaten with 1 tbsp. water. For sweet breads, either a whole egg or egg yolk is beaten with 1 to 2 tbsp. milk or light cream.

Home-style loaves are generally brushed with butter prior to baking and, if a softer crust is preferred, brushed again when the loaves are still warm. Wrapping a loaf with a kitchen towel has the same effect. A few specialty breads and pizzas are brushed lightly with olive oil before baking.

HOME-STYLE HONEY WHEAT BREAD

Scant 1 tbsp. (1 pkg.) active dry yeast
2 cups warm milk (about 110°)
1/4 cup honey
3—4 cups unbleached all-purpose flour

2 cups stone-ground whole wheat flour
1 tbsp. salt
2 tbsps. cooking oil or butter

Melted butter, or egg glaze, page 20.

Dissolve yeast with the milk and honey in a large mixing bowl; let it proof until foamy. Add 1 cup all-purpose flour, whole wheat flour, salt, and cooking oil; beat until smooth. Stir in remaining flour, 1 cup at a time, to make a firm dough. Turn out onto lightly floured board; cover and let rest 10 minutes. Knead until smooth and elastic, adding flour as needed to prevent sticking, about 10 minutes.

Place in a greased bowl and turn to coat the surface. Cover and let rise in a warm place until doubled in size, about 1 1/2 to 2 hours.

Punch down the dough. Shape into 2 loaves, placing in either greased, 9 x 5-inch loaf pans, or on Superstone or cookie sheet sprinkled with wheat germ. Brush with melted butter or egg glaze. Cover and let rise until loaves double in size. Bake in 375° oven for 40 to 45 minutes until loaves sound hollow when tapped. Remove from Superstone onto a rack to cool.

For **Raisin-Nut Bread**, add 1 cup raisins and 1/2 cup finely chopped nuts with the first addition of flour. Frost with Powdered Sugar Icing.

For **Crusty Braided Loaves**, braid, then sprinkle generously with wheat germ or miller's bran after brushing with egg glaze.

For **Sugar Top Loaves**, use all-purpose flour in place of whole wheat flour. Shape dough into round, free-form loaves or braids, or bake part of the dough in baking crocks. Brush loaves with an egg glaze. Sprinkle with about 1/4 cup slivered almonds and 1/4 cup sugar. Crushed sugar cubes or pearl sugar make this particularly festive.

For **Bread Sticks or Pretzels**, follow directions on page 25.

SEVEN-GRAIN WHOLE WHEAT BREAD

The nuttiness of wheat, oats, wheat bran, rye, cornmeal, flax, and psyllium seed spark every bite of this popular sandwich bread. Looking for cereal ingredients like these makes shopping an adventure. Makes two loaves.

1 cup seven-grain cereal
1 cup boiling water
Scant 1 tbsp. (1 pkg.) active dry yeast
2 cups warm water
1/2 cup instant nonfat dry milk
1/3 cup cooking oil
1/4 cup honey
1 tbsp. (3 tsp.) salt
2 cups stone-ground whole wheat flour
5—5½ cups unbleached all-purpose flour

Pour boiling water over seven-grain cereal in a mixing bowl; let cool until lukewarm, about 20 minutes. Dissolve the yeast in warm water in a large mixing bowl. Stir in the cereal mixture, the dry milk, cooking oil, honey, and salt; mix well. Add the whole wheat flour and 1 cup all-purpose flour; beat until smooth. Add enough of the remaining flour to form a firm dough. Turn out onto lightly floured board and knead until smooth, about 10 minutes. Place in a greased bowl and turn to coat the surface. Cover and let rise in a warm place until doubled in size, about 1 1/2 hours.

Punch down the dough. Divide it into 2 portions and shape loaves, placing in either greased 9 x 5-inch loaf pans or on Superstone tile sprinkled with cornmeal.

Cover and let rise until loaves have doubled in size, about an hour.

Bake in a 350° oven for about 40 to 45 minutes, until loaves are nicely browned and sound hollow when tapped. Remove from pan onto a rack to cool.

GRAHAM HEALTH BREAD

Our family's favorite everyday bread, this is also a good bread to use with baking crocks. The Cinnamon-Raisin variation stars at breakfast. Makes two loaves.

Scant 1 tbsp. (1 pkg.) active dry yeast
2 cups warm milk
1/4 cup brown sugar
3 cups graham or whole wheat flour
1/2 cup soy flour (optional)
2 tsp. salt
1/3 cup cooking oil
1/4 cup molasses
3—4 cups unbleached all-purpose flour

Dissolve yeast with the milk and brown sugar in large mixing bowl; let proof until foamy. Add graham and soy flours, salt, cooking oil, and molasses; beat until smooth. Stir in remaining flour, a cup at a time, to make a fairly stiff dough. Turn out onto lightly floured board, cover and let rest

10 minutes. Knead until smooth and elastic, adding flour as needed to prevent sticking, about 10 minutes.

Place dough in a greased bowl and turn to coat the surface. Cover and let rise in a warm place until doubled in size, about 1 1/2 to 2 hours. Punch down the dough, knead a few times, cover and let rise again, about an hour. (If desired, dough can be shaped after a single rise, but the bread will have a coarser texture.)

Punch down the dough. Shape into 2 loaves, placing in greased 9 x 5-inch loaf pans, or on Superstone tile or cookie sheet sprinkled with wheat germ. Cover and let rise until loaves have doubled in size. Bake in 375° oven 40 to 45 minutes until loaves sound hollow when tapped. Remove from Superstone onto a rack to cool.

For **Cinnamon-Raisin Bread**, roll dough into 2 rectangles for pan loaves. Brush with melted butter. In a small bowl, combine 1 cup raisins, 1/2 cup brown sugar, and 2 tbsp. cinnamon. Sprinkle raisin mixture on dough, press in lightly. Shape loaves. Brush baked loaves with melted buter when removed from pans.

BUTTERMILK POTATO BREAD

This old-fashioned loaf, with a marvelous moistness and just a hint of "sourness," was popular with the early pioneers. It was perfect for leftover potatoes and the buttermilk left after churning. This recipe works well in La Cloche. Makes two loaves.

Scant 1 tbsp. (1 pkg.) active dry yeast
1 cup warm potato water or water
3 tbsp. sugar
1 cup mashed potatoes
1 cup buttermilk
1/3 cup butter
7—7 1/2 cups unbleached all-purpose flour
2 tsp. salt

Dissolve the yeast in the potato water and sugar; let it proof. Heat potatoes, buttermilk, and butter until warm, stirring with a whisk until mixture is fairly smooth; let cool. Add to the yeast mixture, along with salt and 2 cups flour; mix well. Stir in 2 more cups flour and beat until smooth. Stir in enough additional flour, a cup at a time, to form a firm dough.

Turn out on a floured board and knead until smooth, adding flour as needed, until dough is smooth and elastic. The stickiness will not completely disappear. Cover and let rise in warm place until doubled in size, about an hour.

Punch down the dough. Shape into 2 loaves, placing either in greased 9 x 5-inch loaf pans or on Superstone sprinkled with cornmeal. Cover and let rise until loaves double in size, about 45 minutes. Sprinkle loaves lightly with flour. Bake in 350° oven for about 45 minutes, until loaves are nicely browned and sound hollow when tapped. Remove from pans onto a rack to cool. Store in the refrigerator.

ANADAMA BREAD

Molasses, whole wheat, and cornmeal were popular ingredients in early American baking. Legend has it this bread came to be when a 19th century fisherman with a very lazy wife took baking into his own hands, all the while muttering, "Anna, damn her." Makes two loaves.

1/2 cup stoneground yellow cornmeal
1 1/2 cups boiling water
1/2 cup molasses
2 tbsp. butter
1 tbsp. salt
Scant 2 tbsp. (2 pkgs.) active dry yeast
1/2 cup warm water
2 cups whole wheat flour
About 4 cups unbleached all-purpose flour

Stir cornmeal into boiling water, add molasses, butter, and salt. Set aside and allow to cool until lukewarm.

Dissolve the yeast in 1/2 cup warm water in large mixing bowl. Stir in the cornmeal mixture and mix well. Add the whole wheat flour and 1 cup all-purpose flour and beat until smooth. Add enough of the remaining flour to form a firm dough. Turn out on a floured board and knead until smooth, about 10 minutes. Place in a greased bowl and turn to coat the surface. Cover and let rise in a warm place until doubled in size, about 1 1/2 hours.

Punch down the dough. Divide into 2 portions and shape loaves, placing in either a greased 9 x 5-inch loaf pans or on Superstone baking stone sprinkled with cornmeal. Cover and let rise until loaves have doubled in size, about an hour.

Bake in 350° oven about 40 to 45 minutes, until loaves are nicely browned and sound hollow when tapped. Remove from pans onto a rack to cool.

CRUSTY COUNTRY ROLLS

Natural stoneware tiles are the key to these Continental-style chewy rolls, bread sticks, and pretzels. Makes about 18 rolls.

Scant 1 tbsp. (1 pkg.) active dry yeast
1 cup warm water
2 tbsp. sugar
3—3 1/4 cups unbleached all-purpose flour
1 tsp. salt
1 tbsp. cooking oil
1 egg

Egg wash, page 20.

Dissolve the yeast with the water and sugar in a large mixing bowl; let it proof until foamy. Add 2 cups flour, salt, cooking oil and egg; beat until smooth. Stir in the remaining flour a little at a time, to make a stiff dough. (If using dough for pretzels, cover tightly and refrigerate. The dough will rise in the refrigerator, without kneading, in about 4 to 6 hours.) Turn out onto lightly floured board and knead until smooth and elastic, about 10 minutes.

Place kneaded dough in a greased bowl and turn to coat the surface. Cover and let rise in a warm place until doubled in size,

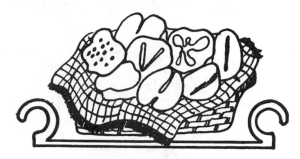

about 1 1/2 hours. Punch down the dough. The dough can be shaped at this point or allowed to rise a second time before shaping. Shape and let rise as directed in the following recipes. Bake in 400° oven for 15 to 20 minutes until golden brown. Remove from Superstone tile onto a rack to cool.

For **Vienna Rolls,** divide the dough into 12 to 18 parts. Shape into balls, then flatten into 5-inch tapered oblongs. Place on Superstone tile or cookie sheet sprinkled with cornmeal. Brush with egg wash. Let rise until doubled, about 20 to 30 minutes. Slash tops with 2 diagonal cuts. Brush again with egg wash and sprinkle with poppy or sesame seeds. Bake.

For **Onion Rolls,** saute 1/4 cup finely chopped onion in 1 tbsp. butter. Stir in 1 tbsp. poppy seeds, and 1/4 teaspoon **each** garlic salt and paprika; set aside. Divide dough into 12 to 18 parts. Shape dough into balls, then flatten into 3-inch circles. Place on Superstone tile or cookie sheet sprinkled with cornmeal. Brush with egg wash. Make an indentation in the center with your fingers. Divide the filling evenly among the rolls. Let the dough rise until it doubles in size. Brush again with egg wash. Bake.

For **Salty Italian Bread Sticks,** divide the dough into 12 to 16 pieces. Roll into 8-inch strands; twist, if desired. Place on Superstone tile or cookie sheet sprinkled with cornmeal. Brush with egg wash. Let the dough rise until puffy. Brush again with egg wash and sprinkle with coarse salt. Bake.

For **Sour Cream Herb Twists,** combine 3 tbsp. sour cream, 2 tbsp. finely minced onion and 1 tbsp. snipped fresh chives; set aside. Turn dough onto lightly oiled surface. Roll to a 10 x 14-inch rectangle. Spread sour cream mixture over dough. Fold rectangle in half to form a 5 x 14-inch rectangle. Cut into 12 5-inch strips. Twist each strip twice and place on greased cookie sheets. Brush lightly with egg wash. Cover and let rise until doubled, about 20 to 30 minutes. Bake.

For **Soft Pretzels,** turn chilled dough onto lightly oiled surface. Divide dough into 16 to 18 parts. Shape each piece into an 18-inch strand. Give each piece a final stretch, and form into pretzel shape on Superstone tile or cookie sheet sprinkled with cornmeal. Brush with egg wash. Cover and let rise in warm place, about 30 minutes. Brush again with egg wash and sprinkle with either coarse salt or sesame seeds. Bake.

For **Large Vienna Crescent,** turn dough onto lightly oiled surface. Roll to a 16-inch square, then fold from one corner to form a triangle. Roll up from long side to opposite point. Transfer to Superstone tile or cookie sheet sprinkled with cornmeal. Shape into crescent. Cover and let rise in warm place until doubled in size, about 45 minutes. Brush with egg wash and sprinkle generously with poppy seeds. Bake for 25 to 30 minutes.

PUMPKIN TOPKNOT LOAF

What a warm and wonderful aroma this has! The pumpkin and spices make it good to eat as a snack while having a cup of tea. This is a particular favorite to accompany a bowl of thick bean soup. Makes one large loaf.

About 3 1/2—4 cups unbleached
　　all-purpose flour
1/2 cup rolled oats
2 tbsp. wheat germ
1 tsp. salt
1/2 tbsp. cinnamon
1/4 tbsp. ginger
1/8 tbsp. nutmeg
Scant 1 tbsp. (1 pkg.) active dry yeast
1 cup warm milk
1 tbsp. honey
1/2 cup mashed pumpkin, squash, or
　　sweet potato
2 tbsp. cooking oil or softened butter
1 egg

Egg glaze, page 20
Additional rolled oats and wheat germ

Combine two cups flour, rolled oats, wheat germ, salt, and spices; set aside. In a large mixing bowl, dissolve yeast in warm milk and honey; let it proof until foamy.

Add pumpkin, cooking oil, and egg to yeast mixture and blend well. Stir in the flour mixture and beat until smooth. Stir in enough remaining flour to form a soft dough. Turn onto a lightly floured board and knead until smooth, adding flour as needed to prevent sticking. Place in a greased bowl and turn to coat the surface. Cover and let rise in a warm place until doubled in size, about an hour.

Punch down the dough and cut off one-third of it. Shape the larger part into a ball and place on Superstone sprinkled with wheat germ. With the heel of your hand, make an indentation in the dough. Shape the remaining dough into a ball, dampen the underside with egg glaze and press on top of the large ball. Brush loaf with egg glaze and sprinkle generously with additional rolled oats and wheat germ.

Cover and let rise until loaf has doubled in size, about 30 to 40 minutes. Bake in a 350° oven about 35 to 40 minutes until golden brown. Remove from Superstone tile onto a rack to cool.

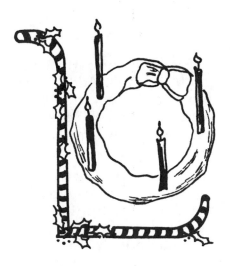

SCANDINAVIAN CARDAMON WREATH

A bread to welcome the Christmas season, this wreath is always baked in our home for St. Lucia's Day, December 13th. Decorate with four red candles when serving at a holiday brunch.

Scant 2 tbsp. (2 pkgs.) active dry yeast
1/2 cup warm water
2/3 cup sugar
1 1/2 tsp. salt
1 1/2 tbsp. freshly ground cardamon
2/3 cup evaporated milk or light cream
2 eggs
1/2 cup softened butter
5—5 1/2 cups unbleached all-purpose flour
1/2 cup light raisins

Egg glaze, page 20

Dissolve yeast in warm water and 1 tbsp. sugar in a large mixing bowl; let it proof until foamy. Add remaining sugar, salt, cardamon, milk, and eggs and blend well. Stir in butter, 3 cups flour and raisins; beat until smooth. Turn out onto lightly floured board and knead until smooth and elastic, adding flour as needed to prevent sticking. Place in a greased bowl and turn to coat the surface. Cover and let rise in a warm place until doubled in size, about 1 1/2 hours.

Turn out onto lightly oiled surface and divide into 3 equal parts. To make a wreath, shape each piece into a 36-inch strand. Braid the strands together, starting at the center and working out. Trim the ends to make them even. Place braid on well seasoned Superstone tile or lightly greased cookie sheet. Shape into a wreath, pinching ends to seal. Roll dough trimmings into a 12-inch strand. Shape into a bow, and place over sealed part of wreath. Brush wreath with egg glaze.

Cover lightly, and let the dough rise until loaf doubles in size, about an hour. Brush again with egg glaze. Bake in 350° oven about 30 to 35 minutes until golden brown. Remove from Superstone onto a rack to cool.

To shape a **Swedish Cardamon Braid,** roll each part of the dough into a strand 10 inches long, tapering the ends. Braid loosely, tucking ends under to seal. Cover lightly, and let the dough rise until the braid doubles in size, about an hour. Brush with egg glaze and bake as directed for wreath.

CHALLAH (HONEY EGG BRAID)

This bread is marvelously light but rich. It is a traditional Jewish Sabbath bread. Saffron, a rare and costly spice, both flavors and colors the bread. A tiny pinch is all that's needed. Makes two braided loaves.

Scant 1 tbsp. (1 pkg.) active dry yeast
1 cup warm water
1/4 cup honey
3 eggs
1 tsp. salt
Pinch saffron (optional)
4—4 1/2 cups unbleached
   all-purpose flour
1/4 cup cooking oil

Egg wash, made with reserved egg and 1
   tbsp. water
Poppy seed

Combine the yeast with warm water and honey in a large mixing bowl, allow to proof until foamy, about 5 minutes. Lightly beat eggs, reserve 2 tbsp. for egg wash. Stir remaining eggs, salt, and saffron into yeast mixture and blend well. Add one cup flour and oil; beat until smooth. Add enough remaining flour to make a soft dough. Cover and let rest in a warm place for about 30 minutes.

Turn out on a floured board and knead a few times until dough is easy to handle and no longer sticky. Knead until smooth and elastic, adding as little flour as necessary to make a soft tender dough. Place in a greased bowl and turn to coat the surface. Cover and let rise in a warm place until doubled in size.

Punch down the dough, and turn out onto lightly oiled surface. Divide the dough in half, then divide each half into 4 pieces. Cover and let rest 10 minutes. To make a loaf, roll 3 pieces of dough into 14-inch strands. Braid the strands together, starting at the center and working out; tuck ends under to secure. Place on greased Superstone tile. Divide remaining piece of dough into thirds; roll each piece into 12-inch strands. Braid the strands together; place on top of the larger braid. Repeat braiding process with remaining dough to form a second loaf.

Brush loaves with egg wash. Let rise in a warm place until almost doubled in size, then brush again with egg wash and sprinkle with poppy seeds. Bake in 375° oven for 25 to 30 minutes until golden brown. Remove from Superstone tile onto a rack to cool.

Sourdough Bread And Starters

Say sourdough bread, and people are reminded of the West and Northwest, of the Goldrush, of miners, trappers and pioneers far from the convenience of grocery stores. Stories of a cherished bit of sourdough starter being carried along as insurance against months of existence on hard "trail" biscuits abound in the lore of this period. Like much of the Old West, sourdough breads have been popularized far beyond their humble origin. Sourdough breads are so popular, in fact, that many people pay outrageous sums to buy them when making them is fairly simple.

Sourdough breads are leavened with a fermented flour mixture used as a starter. Starters can be made in a number of ways, with purists relying on the wild yeasts that are present as a natural part of our environment. These work with varying degrees of success, being best suited for regions of the country with lots of warmth and natural humidity. Living in a more northerly climate, and invariably getting the urge for sourdough bread sometime in January's "soup season," my luck's been better with a yeast-assisted starter.

To get the starter going, its ingredients are mixed together and allowed to set for a day or two, thus activating the fermenting process. As the starter ferments, it increases in volume, gets bubbly, and gives off a pungent, yeasty, slightly sour aroma.

When the starter is ready, it can either be used for one of the following recipes or stored in a covered jar or crock in the refrigerator for use at another time. It's important that the starter be at room temperature when it's used. However, be sure some of it is saved to keep the next batch of starter going.

One of the things I like about using sourdough starter is that a sponge-type batter is used for mixing the dough. While it takes several hours for the batter to develop, it's not time that requires my involvement. This step can take place in the morning for evening baking, or vice versa, and has even been extended by an overnight period in the refrigerator. The batter also serves as a means of replenishing the starter, a step necessary for keeping the yeast alive and active. The recipes that follow all use this method, which also seems to give the most typical "sourdough" flavor and aroma.

Sourdough starter can be used alone as leavening in the following recipes. Some additional yeast has been suggested, as the sourdough works slowly, particularly in breads made with whole grain flour. Once you start working with sourdough starter you may want to omit the yeast; just count on letting the dough rise at least twice as long as usual.

Because sourdough breads are typical of early baking, I've enjoyed completing the process by baking the bread in free-form loaves directly on a preheated Superstone baking stone or baking tiles. Much of what's liked about sourdough bread is its chewy crustiness, so baking on the tiles is a natural. My "hands down" favorite, however, is the Sourdough Irish Oatmeal Bread baked "undercover." This recipe is in the La Cloche chapter.

SOURDOUGH STARTER

Sourdough starters that contain yeast sometimes contain milk, or have added honey or sugar, to "feed" the yeast. These starters, while fine for pancakes, quick breads, and even "home-style" pan loaves, didn't produce the crusty, light, golden loaves of French-style breads that I prefer. The addition of plain yogurt in this starter is a compromise that assures consistent results.

1 cup warm water (about 110°)
Scant 1 tbsp. (1 pkg.) active dry yeast
1 1/2 cups unbleached all-purpose flour
1/2 cup unflavored plain yogurt

Combine yeast with the water in a warm stoneware or glass mixing bowl. With a wooden spoon, stir to dissolve the yeast. Add the flour and yogurt; beat until blended. Cover with plastic wrap and let stand in a warm place (85°) for 36 to 48 hours. Since the mixture expands a bit, make sure the bowl or crock you use is large enough. Starter will develop a sour yeasty aroma, be bubbly, and have a consistency somewhat like pancake batter. Store the starter tightly covered in the refrigerator.

SOURDOUGH STARTER BATTER

Sourdough starter batter is prepared the day before bread is to be baked. Then on baking day you're ready to proceed much as for any yeast bread.

Sourdough starter, page 30
1 1/2 cups unbleached all-purpose flour
1 cup water, room temperature

Let refrigerated sourdough starter come to room temperature. Measure out 1 1/2 cups of the starter into a warm bowl. (Return remaining starter to the refrigerator.) Add flour and water to starter; blend well. Cover and let proof in a warm place (85°) for 8 to 12 hours. Mixture will again appear bubbly, and develop a pungent yeasty aroma. Stir the mixture, and measure out 2 cups for use in any of the following sourdough recipes.

Return remaining mixture to the starter being refrigerated; stir to blend well. This addition replenishes the batter until it is used again, or for about 10 days. (If you do not use the sourdough starter in that time, replenish by adding 1 cup each flour and water, then let the starter stand until bubbly. Refrigerate.)

SOURDOUGH FRENCH BREAD

Makes two loaves

2 tsp. (about 1 pkg.) active dry yeast
1 cup warm water
3 tbsp. sugar
2 cups sourdough starter batter
4—5 cups unbleached all-purpose flour
1 tsp. salt

Egg glaze, page 20

Combine yeast with warm water and sugar in a large mixing bowl; let proof until foamy. Add sourdough batter, about 4 cups flour and salt. Mix to form a stiff dough. Cover and let rest about 20 minutes. Turn out onto lightly floured board and knead, adding flour as needed, until dough is smooth and elastic, about 10 minutes. Place dough in a greased bowl and turn to coat the surface. Cover and let rise in a warm place until doubled in size, about 1 1/2 hours.

Punch down the dough. Shape into 2 free-form loaves and let rise on a cookie sheet with cornmeal, until almost doubled in size, about 45 minutes.

About 15 minutes prior to baking the loaves, preheat the oven and Superstone baking stone or baking tiles to 350°. Slash tops of loaves deeply with sharp knife or scissors, and brush loaves with egg glaze. When loaves are ready, extend the rack holding the tiles, and carefully slide the loaves onto the tiles. Bake at 350° for 40 to 45 minutes until loaves sound hollow when tapped. Remove loaves from oven onto a rack to cool.

SOURDOUGH RYE BREAD

Sourdough rye is a Scandinavian favorite, and this doughnut-shaped loaf is often seen in bakeries, particularly in Finland. The Onion-Rye Bread variation goes well with barbecued hamburgers and steak served with potato salad. Makes two round loaves.

Scant 1 tbsp. (1 pkg.) active dry yeast
1 cup warm water
1/4 cup brown sugar
2 cups sourdough starter batter
2 cups rye flour
3—3 1/2 cups unbleached
   all-purpose flour

1 tbsp. (3tsp.) salt
1 tsp. anise seed
1 tsp. caraway seed
1/4 cup butter

Egg wash, made with 1 beaten egg with
   1 tbsp. water

Combine yeast with warm water and brown sugar in large mixing bowl; let proof until foamy. Add sourdough batter, rye flour, 2 cups all-purpose flour, and remaining ingredients, mixing to form a stiff dough. Turn out onto lightly floured board and knead, adding more flour as needed, until dough is smooth and elastic, about 10 to 15 minutes. Place dough in a greased bowl and turn to coat the surface. Cover and let rise in a warm place until doubled in size, about an hour.

Punch down the dough. Shape into 2 free-form loaves by shaping dough into a ball and placing it on a cookie sheet sprinkled with cornmeal. Roll or pat dough into a circle about 8 to 10 inches in diameter. Poke a hole in the center and stretch the hole to 2 inches in diameter, making loaf into a doughnut shape. Cover and let rise until doubled in size.

About 15 minutes prior to baking the loaves, preheat the oven and baking tiles to 375°. Brush the loaves with egg wash. When loaves are ready, extend the rack holding the tiles and carefully slide the loaves onto them. Bake at 375° for 35 to 40 minutes until loaves sound hollow when tapped. Remove loaves from tiles onto a rack to cool.

For **Sourdough Onion Rye Bread**, shape dough into 2 round loaves. Cover and let rise. When loaves are brushed with egg wash, top loaves with 1 medium onion, finely chopped, and sprinkle with additional caraway seed.

Pizzas and Meat Pastries

Just about everyone likes pizza. The combination of yeast dough crust, fresh tomato sauce, and other delectable ingredients makes for unlimited possibilities.

Sassafras has published the book on pizza with Louise Love's, **The Complete Book of Pizza**. What's offered here are some traditional winning combinations using hearty, and readily available, country ingredients.

The meat pastries included here are a hearty answer to the question, "What's for lunch?" Perfect for picnics, they're also ideal for sporting events, hikes or sailing. They'll stay warm, wrapped in foil in an insulated bag, for two to three hours.

BASIC PIZZA CRUST

Makes one crust

Scant 1 tbsp. (1 pkg.) active dry yeast
1 cup warm water (about 110°)
1 tsp. sugar
2 3/4—3 cups unbleached
    all-purpose flour
1 tsp. salt
1 tbsp. olive oil

In a mixing bowl, dissolve yeast in the water with the sugar. Add about 1 cup flour with the salt and oil; beat well. Add enough additional flour to make a stiff dough. Turn out onto lightly floured board and knead for about 10 minutes, adding flour as needed, until dough is smooth and elastic. Place in a greased bowl and turn to coat the surface. Cover and let rise in a warm place until doubled in size, about 1 1/2 hours. (Or, to make ahead; refrigerate covered dough and allow to rise 8 to 12 hours, or overnight. Let stand at room temperature 30 minutes before using.)

Punch down the dough. Cover and let rest 15 to 20 minutes. On a floured surface, roll out dough to a circle slightly larger than a Superstone, about 14 inches.

For a **Superstone Pizza**, place the dough on a Superstone sprinkled with cornmeal, shaping edges of the dough to form a rim. Brush lightly with olive oil, if desired. Top with one of the fillings that follow or create your own. Bake in 450° oven 20 to 25 minutes until crust is golden and filling is bubbly.

For **Brick Oven Pizza**, place dough on a pizza paddle (or peel) sprinkled with cornmeal. (A cookie sheet will also work.) Shape the edges of the dough to form a rim on the crust, brush lightly with additional olive oil. Let the crust rise for 15 to 20 minutes while oven and Superstone baking stone or baking tiles are preheating to 450°. This gives a better foundation for filling ingredients, and eases sliding the assembled pizza onto the Superstone baking stone. Top with one of the fillings that follow or create your own. Extend the oven rack holding the Superstone and carefully slide the pizza onto the tile. Bake at 450° for 20 to 25 minutes until crust is golden and filling is bubbly.

FRESH TOMATO SAUCE FOR PIZZA

When fresh tomatoes aren't available, use two 28-ounce cans of Italian plum tomatoes for this recipe. "Hothouse" tomatoes never work in cooking this thick wonderful sauce. If you like a smooth sauce, puree the cooled sauce in a food processor, blender, or food mill. Makes one and a half to two quarts.

    1/4 cup olive oil, or part oil and
        part butter
    4 medium onions, chopped
        (about 2 cups)
    2 cloves garlic, minced
    3 pounds Italian plum or "meaty"
        tomatoes, peeled, seeded, coarsely
        chopped and well drained
    2 tbsp. chopped fresh basil
    2 tbsp. chopped fresh oregano
    2 tsp. sugar
    Salt and freshly ground pepper
    1 can (6 oz.) tomato paste

Heat oil in a large heavy saucepan; add onions and garlic. Cook until soft, without browning the vegetable. Stir in remaining ingredients. Simmer the sauce, partially covered, 45 to 60 minutes, stirring often. Taste, and adjust seasoning if needed, allowing for seasonings in the pizza's filling ingredients. Let cool, and divide into 1 1/2 cup portions. These can be refreigerated for a week or so, or frozen for several months.

TRADITIONAL CHEESE AND TOMATO PIZZA

There aren't many times when this would be my pizza choice, except that the Fresh Tomato Sauce is so tasty on its own, particularly when enhanced with extra fresh basil and oregano. Nothing in this pizza will hide the taste of the very best ingredients. It's also good with a whole wheat crust. Just substitute 1 cup whole wheat flour for 1 cup all-purpose flour. Makes one 12 inch pizza.

    Basic Pizza Crust, page 33
    1 1/2 cups fresh tomato Sauce
    3/4 to 1 lb. shredded mozzarella cheese
    1 cup freshly grated parmesan cheese
    Olive oil.

Prepare pizza crust. Spread tomato sauce over unbaked crust. Sprinkle with half the mozzarella cheese, then combine remaining mozzarella and parmesan cheese. Sprinkle over first layer. Drizzle with a little olive oil. Bake in 450° oven 20 to 25 minutes until crust is golden and filling is bubbly.

PEPPERONI, HAM, AND MUSHROOM PIZZA

Makes one 12 inch pizza

Basic Pizza Crust, page 33
1 cup (1/2 pt.) sliced fresh mushrooms
2 tbsp. butter
1 1/2 cups Fresh Tomato Sauce, page 34
1/2 lb. pepperoni, thinly sliced
1/2 lb. thinly sliced ham, shredded
1/2 lb. shredded Mozzarella cheese
1/4 to 1/2 cup freshly grated
    parmesan cheese

Prepare pizza crust. Lightly saute mushrooms in butter. Spread tomato sauce over unbaked crust. Add the pepperoni, ham, and mushrooms. Sprinkle with cheeses. Bake in 450° oven 20 to 25 minutes until crust is golden and filling is bubbly.

SALAMI ON RYE PIZZA

Makes one 12 inch pizza

Basic Pizza Crust, prepared with
    1 1/2 cups rye flour for 1 1/2 cups
    all-purpose flour, page 33
1 1/2 cups Fresh Tomato Sauce, page 34
1/4 pound sliced salami, cut in quarters
1 medium onion, sliced
Sweet red or green pepper, cut in strips
    (about 1/2 large)
1/2 pound shredded Monterey Jack
    cheese
1/4 to 1/2 cup freshly grated parmesan
    cheese

Prepare pizza crust. Spread tomato sauce over unbaked crust. Add the salami, onion and pepper. Sprinkle with cheeses. Bake in 450° oven 20 to 25 minutes until crust is golden and filling is bubbly.

PICK-ME-UP SANDWICH BUNS

A light rye bun encases two fillings to make ideal take-along sandwiches. Both fillings can be made ahead of time and, when cooled and wrapped airtight, either refrigerated or frozen. Thaw before reheating.

Scant 1 tbsp. (1 pkg.) active dry yeast
1 cup warm water
1/4 cup brown sugar
3/4 tsp. salt
1/4 cup cooking oil
1 egg
1 1/2—2 cups unbleached all-purpose flour
2 cups rye flour
1/3 cup wheat germ

Dissolve yeast in warm water in large mixing bowl. Add sugar, salt, cooking oil, and egg. In another bowl, combine 1 1/2 cups all-purpose flour, rye flour, and wheat germ. Add about 2 cups of the flour mixture to the yeast mixture; beat until smooth. Stir in enough of the remaining flour, adding a little at a time, to make a medium-stiff dough. Turn out onto lightly floured board and knead until smooth and elastic, adding flour as needed to prevent sticking, about 10 minutes. Place in a greased bowl and turn to coat the surface. Cover and let rise in a warm place until doubled in size, about 2 hours.

Punch down the dough. Shape and bake as directed in recipes for Pick-Me-Up Krautburgers and Pick-Me-Up Ham and Cheese Turnovers.

PICK-ME-UP KRAUTBURGERS

This family recipe, here in a rye bun with cheese added, was a "hoped for" luncheon treat when visiting one of my aunts. Made by the dozens for her church's fund-raisers, these hearty buns have a Reuben sandwich taste. Makes 10 sandwich buns.

Pick-Me-Up Sandwich Buns

1 lb. lean ground beef
2 medium onions, chopped
Salt and pepper
1/2 small cabbbage, shredded
  (about 1/2 lb.)
2 cups (8 oz.) shredded Swiss or
  Monterrey Jack cheese
2 tsp. caraway seed

Prepare sandwich buns. While the dough rises, brown ground beef with onions in a large skillet over medium heat; season with salt and pepper. Add cabbage, cover, and cook over low heat until cabbage is tender, about 10 minutes. Let cool slightly. Stir in cheese and caraway seed.

Roll out dough on a lightly oiled surface and form a 10 x 25 inch rectangle. Cut the dough into 10 squares, each 5 x 5 inches. Spoon filling into the center of each square, dividing evenly. Bring up corners of the dough, forming an envelope shape, pinching edges to seal securely. Place Krautburgers on Superstone tile, or cookie sheet sprinkled with cornmeal. Prick tops of buns with a fork. Cover lightly and let rise in warm place until puffy, about 20 to 30 minutes.

Bake in 375° oven for 15 to 20 minutes until golden brown. Remove from Superstone tile onto a rack to cool.

PICK-ME-UP HAM AND CHEESE TURNOVERS

Made with ricotta and mozzarella cheeses, and wrapped with pizza dough, these become Italian turnovers called calzone. Makes eight turnovers.

Pick-Me-Up Sandwich Buns, page 36, or Basic Pizza Dough, page 33.

1 cup (8 oz.) ricotta or farmer's cheese
1 cup thinly sliced ham, shredded
   (about 1/4 lb.)
1 cup (4 oz.) shredded mozzarella or
   Swiss cheese
1 small bunch (about 1/4 lb.) fresh
   spinach, cooked, drained, squeezed dry,
   and chopped
2 tsp. chopped fresh basil, oregano,
   or rosemary

Prepare sandwich buns. Combine remaining ingredients and mix well. Divide the dough into 8 equal parts. Shape each piece into a ball, then flatten and roll into a 6-inch circle. Place one-eighth of the filling in the center of each circle, then fold circle in half, pressing edges together to seal securely. Place turnovers on Superstone or cookie sheet sprinkled with cornmeal. Make 2 short slashes in each turnover with a sharp knife or scissors. Cover lightly and let rise in

warm place until puffy, about 20 to 30 minutes. Bake in 375° oven for 15 to 20 minutes until golden brown. Remove from Superstone tile onto a rack to cool.

Biscuits And Scones

If any bread fits the name "quick" bread, these do. Not only are they baked in a jiffy, but handling the dough calls for a quick, light touch.

The mixture is combined like pastry (for directions, see page 82) and kneaded for a very short time like bread (for directions, see page 17).

While regular biscuits baked quickly at high temperatures don't benefit greatly by baking on tiles, these richer versions do. Served right from the Superstone tile, biscuits stay warmer longer than when baked on cookie sheets.

WHOLEWHEAT CURRANT SCONES

Whether for morning coffee or afternoon tea, these English delights are a treat to serve with butter and jam. Makes four to six servings.

1 cup unbleached all-purpose flour
1 cup whole wheat flour
1 tbsp. baking powder
1/4 cup sugar
1/4 tsp. salt
1/3 cup butter
2 eggs, lightly beaten
1/3 cup milk
1/2 cup currants
2 tbsp. sugar with 1/2 tsp. cinnamon

Combine flours, baking powder, sugar and salt in a mixing bowl. With a pastry blender, cut in the butter until mixture resembles coarse crumbs. Reserve 2 tbsp. beaten egg. Stir remaining egg, milk, and currants into flour mixture just until particles cling together. Turn out onto lightly floured board and knead 6 to 10 times. On greased Superstone tile, pat into a circle about 3/4 inch thick. Cut into 8 wedges; keep wedges slightly apart so that they have room to rise.

Brush reserved egg over tops of the wedges and sprinkle with cinnamon and sugar mixture. Bake in a 425° oven for 18 to 20 minutes until browned. Serve piping hot.

BEEF AND CHEESE BISCUIT WEDGES

Whether as a snacking bread with a mug of beer, or to have with a rich vegetable soup, these wedges are quick to make and quick to disappear. Makes four to six servings.

2 cups unbleached all-purpose flour
1 tbsp. baking powder
1 tbsp. sugar
1/2 cup thinly sliced smoked beef, cut in small pieces
1 cup shredded colby or cheddar cheese
1 small (1/4 cup) finely chopped onion
1 cup sour cream
1/4 cup water

Stir dry ingredients together. Stir in the beef, 1/2 cup of the cheese, and the onion. Fold in the sour cream and water until particles cling together. Turn out on lightly floured board and knead for about one minute. On a Superstone tile sprinkled with cornmeal, pat the dough into a circle about 3/4 inch thick. Cut into 8 wedges, keeping wedges slightly apart so that they have room to rise.

Bake in a 400° oven for 20 minutes, or until light brown, then sprinkle with remaining cheese. Continue baking until golden brown and cheese has melted, about 5 to 10 minutes. Serve very hot.

Cookies, Cookies, Cookies

Cookies are the first thing that most of us learn to bake. Our country kitchen table was often covered with them, the results of a whole afternoon of baking. There were a variety of cookies to eat, with some to share and others to freeze for later. Mostly they were hearty drop cookies chocked full of raisins, nuts, cereals, and chocolate chips. These varieties are all good for Superstone baking.

What follow are some personal favorites. Many of these have been modified over the years so that they have less sugar and more whole-grain goodness. Drop cookies are fairly basic, and they can be a beginning for your own "sneaky" nutritional inventiveness.

SPICY GINGER COOKIES

Makes 48 cookies.

1 cup brown sugar
1/2 cup shortening, softened butter,
    or margarine
1/4 cup water
1/4 cup molasses

2 eggs
2 1/2 cups whole wheat flour
1 tsp. baking soda
1/2 tsp. ginger
1/2 tsp. cloves
1/2 tsp. cinnamon
Wheat germ

Combine sugar, shortening, water, molasses, and eggs in a large bowl; blend well. Stir in remaining ingredients (except wheat germ) until well blended. Cover and chill at least 2 hours, or overnight.

Shape into 1-inch balls. Roll each ball in wheat germ and place 2 inches apart on a well seasoned Superstone tile or greased cookie sheets.

Bake in a 350° oven for 10 to 12 minutes until golden brown. Remove the cookies from the Superstone tile and place them onto a rack to cool.

DOUBLE PEANUT BLOSSOMS

Makes 48 cookies.

1 cup brown sugar
1/2 cup granulated sugar
3/4 cup shortening, softened butter,
    or margarine
1/2 cup peanut butter
1 tsp. vanilla
1 egg
2 cups unbleached all-purpose flour
1 tsp. baking powder
2 cups chow mein noodles,
    coarsely crushed
1 11-ounce box (48 candies) bite-size
    chocolate-covered peanut buttercup
    candies

Combine sugars, shortening, baking powder, vanilla, and egg in large bowl; blend until smooth. Stir in flour and baking powder; blend well. Stir in chow mein noodles. Shape into 1-inch balls and place 2 inches apart on well seasoned Superstone tile or cookie sheets. Make a large depression in the center of each cookie.

Bake in 375° oven for 8 minutes. Press a candy into each center. Bake 2 to 3 minutes more. Cool a few minutes, then remove from Superstone tile and place onto a rack to cool.

OATMEAL PEANUT BUTTER COOKIES

Makes 48 to 60 cookies

1 cup brown sugar
1 cup shortening, softened butter,
    or margarine
1/2 cup peanut butter
1/2 cup honey
1/4 cup milk
1 egg
1 1/2 cup unbleached
    all-purpose flour
2 tbsp. wheat germ
1 tsp. baking soda
1 tsp. cinnamon
3 cups rolled oats
1/2 cup sunflower nuts or
    chopped peanuts

Combine sugar, shortening, peanut butter, honey, milk, and egg in large bowl; blend until smooth. Stir in flour, wheat germ, baking soda, and cinnamon; blend well. Stir in oats and sunflower nuts. Drop by rounded teasponfuls, 2 inches apart, onto well seasoned Superstone tile or greased cookie sheets.

Bake in a 375° oven for 14 to 18 minutes until golden brown. Remove the cookies from Superstone tile and place onto a rack to cool.

SUNNY CARROT COOKIES

Chewy bits of coconut and crunchy sunflower seeds dot this moist cake-like cookie. Makes 48 to 54 cookies.

3/4 cup brown sugar
1 cup shortening, softened
   butter, or margarine
1—1 1/4 cups mashed cooked carrots
2 eggs
1 cup whole wheat flour
1 cup unbleached all-purpose flour
2 tsp. baking powder
1/2 tsp. salt
1 cup shredded coconut
1/2 cup sunflower nuts

Combine sugar, shortening, carrots, and eggs in a large bowl; blend until smooth. Stir in flours, baking powder and salt; blend well. Stir in coconut and sunflower nuts. Drop by rounded teaspoonfuls, 2 inches apart, onto well seasoned Superstone tile or lightly greased cookie sheet.

Bake in a 375° oven for 12 to 14 minutes until golden brown and no imprint remains when cookies are lightly touched with a finger. Remove the cookies from Superstone tile and place onto a rack to cool.

SALTED PEANUT COOKIES

Makes 48 to 60 cookies.

1 1/2 cups brown sugar
1 cup shortening, softened
   butter, or margarine
1 tsp. vanilla
2 eggs
2 cups unbleached all-purpose flour
1 tsp. baking soda
1 tsp. baking powder
1 cup rolled oats
2 cups cereal flakes, finely crushed
1 cup salted peanuts, coarsely
   chopped

Combine brown sugar, shortening, vanilla, and eggs in large bowl; blend until smooth. Stir in flour, baking soda and baking powder; blend well. Stir in remaining ingredients. Drop by heaping teaspoonfuls, 2 inches apart, onto well seasoned Superstone tile or greased cookie sheets.

Bake in a 375° oven for 12 to 15 minutes until light brown. Remove the cookies from Superstone tile and place onto a rack to cool.

WHOLE WHEAT CHOCOLATE CHIP COOKIES

Carob chips are available in health food stores, and are often used instead of chocolate chips. Makes 40 to 48 cookies.

1 1/2 cups brown sugar
1 cup shortening, softened
    butter, or margarine
1 tsp. vanilla
2 eggs
1 1/2 cups whole wheat flour

1 cup unbleached all-purpose flour
1 1/2 tsp. baking soda
1—2 cups (6 or 12 oz. pkgs.)
    semi-sweet chocolate chips
3/4 cup chopped nuts

Combine brown sugar, shortening, vanilla, and eggs in large bowl; blend until smooth. Stir in flours and baking soda; blend well. Stir in remaining ingredients. Drop by heaping teaspoonfuls, 2 inches apart, onto well seasoned Superstone tile or greased cookie sheets.

Bake in a 375° oven for 10 to 14 minutes until light brown. Remove the cookies from Superstone tile and place onto a rack to cool.

CHAPTER TWO
SUPERSTONE™
FRENCH BREAD BAKER

A crusty French baguette with light open texture, the goal of many a bread baker, is hard to achieve at home. But the Superstone French Bread Baker is helpful because of its shape and the natural stoneware from which it's made.

Several cookbooks, particularly Julia Child and Simone Beck's, **Mastering the Art of French Cooking, Volume 2,** explain the techniques for perfect French bread in detail. There are three recipes in this book that are easier versions of French-style breads: the Simple French Bread in this chapter, the Sourdough French Bread in the Superstone chapter, and the Crusty Country Loaves in the La Cloche chapter.

Some of the keys to classic French breads are important for these loaves as well. First, use a bread flour, if possible, as it has more gluten than an all-purpose flour. Add only as much flour as absolutely necessary for mixing and kneading, as French bread dough is soft. Knead the dough for as long as you can, 15 minutes is typical. Long, slow rising allows for easier shaping. These are bread doughs that shouldn't be pushed to rise at more than normal room temperature. Some people suggest not making this type of bread on a hot day.

Because French bread is made from just yeast, flour, water, and salt, it is best eaten on the same day that it's made; it gets stale quickly. Loaves can be frozen to preserve freshness. To use, unwrap and thaw by placing directly on oven racks in a 350° oven for 10 to 15 minutes.

The French Bread Baker is fun to use for other long bread loaves. We often enjoy savory loaves with party-sliced meats, cheeses, and barbecued foods.

Shaping directions given in the bread-making section of the Superstone chapter will spark additional shaping ideas, as will a visit to a bakery that specializes in French Bread.

To make these recipes without the French Bread Baker, simply shape on a Superstone baking stone or cookie sheet. When using a cookie sheet, oven temperatures should be set about 25° higher than indicated.

SIMPLE FRENCH BREAD

The method used to bake this bread is one that raises the eyebrows of experienced bakers. It makes a good French-style bread, however, and is the method used for the crusty Cuban breads that are popular in South Florida. Makes two long loaves.

1 tbsp. (1 1/2 pkgs.) active dry yeast
2 cups warm water
1 tbsp. honey
6—7 cups bread flour or
    unbleached all-purpose flour
1 tbsp. salt

Egg glaze, page 20

Combine yeast with water and honey in large mixing bowl; let proof until foamy. Add 5 cups flour and salt to the yeast mixture, mixing to form a stiff dough. Turn out onto lightly floured board and knead at least 10 minutes, adding flour as needed to prevent sticking. Dough should be very smooth and elastic. Place in a greased bowl and turn to coat the surface. Cover and let rise in a warm place until doubled in size, about 1 1/2 hours.

Punch down the dough. Shape into 2 long loaves and place on a French Bread Baker sprinkled with cornmeal. Cover and let the dough rise until loaves have doubled in size, about an hour. Slash the tops deeply with a sharp knife or scissors; brush with egg glaze. Place in a cold oven. Set the temperature at 400° and bake for 30 to 40 minutes, until loaves sound hollow when tapped. Remove from French Bread Baker and place onto a rack to cool.

ITALIAN SESAME LOAVES

The nuttiness of sesame and the flavor of olive oil make a pleasing variation to this basic crusty loaf. A quality olive oil is always the key. Makes two long loaves.

1 tbsp. (1 1/2 pkgs.) active dry yeast
1 1/2 cups warm water
1 tsp. sugar
4 1/2—5 cups bread flour or
    unbleached all-purpose flour
1/3 cup sesame seed
2 tsp. salt
2 tbsp. olive oil

Olive oil
Sesame seed

Combine the yeast with warm water and sugar in a large mixing bowl; let proof until foamy. In a bowl, combine 4 cups flour, the sesame seed and salt. Add flour mixture and the olive oil to the yeast mixture, mixing to form a stiff dough. Turn out onto a lightly floured board and knead for about 10 minutes, adding flour as needed, until dough is smooth. Place in a greased bowl and turn to coat the surface. Cover and let rise in a warm place until doubled in size, about an hour.

Punch down the dough. Shape into two long loaves and place on a French Bread Baker sprinkled with cornmeal. Brush loaves lightly with olive oil and sprinkle with sesame seed. Let dough rise, uncovered, until loaves have almost doubled in size, about 45 minutes. Slash the tops deeply with a sharp knife or scissors. Place in a cold oven. Set the temperature at 400°

and bake for 30 to 40 minutes, until loaves sound hollow when tapped. Remove from French Bread Baker and place onto a rack to cool.

TWO-TONE RYE PARTY BREAD

A favorite for parties, this variation of Swedish Limpa and Pumpernickel is easy to slice into paper thin slices for a sandwich board. Every slice looks different! Makes two long loaves.

3—3 1/2 cups unbleached
   all-purpose flour
3 cups rye flour
Scant 1 tbsp. (1 pkg.) active dry yeast
2 cups warm water
1/3 cup molasses
1/4 cup softened butter
1 tbsp. salt
1 tbsp. grated orange peel
2 tbsp. cocoa
2 tsp. anise or caraway seed
1 tsp. instant coffee powder

Egg glaze, page 20

Combine 3 cups all-purpose flour and the rye flour; set aside. In a large mixing bowl, dissolve the yeast in the warm water. Stir in the molasses, butter, salt, orange peel, and 2 cups of the flour mixture. Beat to blend, then beat for several more minutes. Pour half the batter into another bowl.

To batter remaining in the mixing bowl, stir in cocoa, anise seed, instant coffee, and 1 1/2 more cups of the flour mixture. Turn out onto a board and knead until smooth, adding additional flour as needed to prevent sticking.

To second batter, stir in enough remaining flour to make a stiff dough. Turn out onto a board and knead until smooth, adding additional all-purpose flour as needed to prevent sticking.

Place each dough into a greased bowl, and turn each to coat the surface. Cover and let rise in a warm place until doubled in size, about an hour.

Punch down the doughs and divide each into equal halves. Roll each portion into a smooth 14-inch strand. For each loaf, twist a dark and a light strand together, tucking ends underneath to seal. Place loaves on a French Bread Baker sprinkled with cornmeal. Cover lightly and let rise until doubled in size, about 45 minutes.

Brush both loaves with egg glaze. Bake in a 350° oven for about 25 to 30 minutes, or until well browned. Remove from French Bread Baker and place onto a rack to cool.

DOUBLE CHEESE BREAD TWISTS

Cheese-flavored breads are the ones we like with succulent barbecued ribs! Makes two long loaves.

1 tbsp. (1 1/2 pkgs.) active dry yeast
1 1/2 cups warm water
2 tbsp. sugar
1/3 cup freshly grated parmesan cheese
3/4 cup shredded Swiss cheese

1/4 cup wheat germ or miller's bran
1/4 cup softened butter
4 1/2—5 cups unbleached
    all-purpose flour

Melted butter

Dissolve yeast in warm water and sugar; let it proof about 5 minutes. Reserve 2 tbsp. parmesan cheese. Add remaining parmesan cheese to yeast mixture along with Swiss cheese, wheat germ, butter, and 2 cups flour; beat until smooth. Stir in enough of the remaining flour to make a soft dough. Turn out onto lightly floured board and knead until smooth and elastic, adding flour as needed to prevent sticking. Place in a greased bowl and turn to coat the surface. Cover and let rise in a warm place until doubled in size.

Punch down the dough and divide into 4 equal parts. Roll each portion into a smooth 14-inch strand. For each loaf, twist 2 strands together, tucking ends underneath to seal. Place loaves on a French Bread Baker sprinkled with cornmeal. Brush with melted butter and sprinkle with remaining parmesan cheese. Let rise until doubled in size. Bake in a 350° oven for 35 to 40 minutes until golden brown. Remove from French Bread Baker and place onto a rack to cool. Loaves may be lightly brushed with more melted butter.

HERB-FILLED SOUR CREAM LOAVES

An herb grower's delight, this light and tender sour cream loaf will highlight a simple meal. Try it with egg dishes, seafood salads, or a bean-filled cassoulet. Makes two long loaves.

Scant 1 tbsp. (1 pkg.) active dry yeast
1/2 cup warm water
2 tbsp. sugar
1 cup sour cream
1/2 cup butter
2 eggs

1 tsp. salt
5 1/2—6 cups unbleached
   all-purpose flour
Herb filling, below
Egg glaze, page 20

Dissolve the yeast in the water with the sugar, let it proof. Heat sour cream and butter until mixture is very warm and butter melts; let cool. Add to yeast mixture along with eggs and salt; mix well. Stir in 2 cups flour and beat until smooth. Gradually add remaining flour and mix until a soft dough is formed.

Turn out on lightly floured board and knead until dough is easy to handle, and has a smooth velvety appearence. Cover and let rest for about 20 minutes, or while preparing herb filling.

Divide dough into 2 equal parts and roll each into a rectangle, about 12 x 14 inches. Spread each rectangle to within an inch of the edge with the herb filling. Roll up from the wide end, jelly-roll fashion. Seal edges. Place, sealed edges down, on French Bread Baker that has been sprinkled with cornmeal. Cover and let rise until loaves have doubled in size, about an hour.

Brush with egg glaze, and slash the tops deeply in 3 or 4 places with a sharp knife or scissors. Bake in a 350° oven for about 30 minutes, until loaves sound hollow when tapped. Remove loaves from French Bread Baker and place onto a rack to cool.

For **Herb Filling:** Melt 1/4 cup butter. Stir in 1/4 cup chopped fresh parsley, 2 tbsps. **each** chopped fresh dill and snipped fresh chives, and 1 tsp. seasoned salt.

49

Baking crocks make baking fun by introducing a different shape to the process. They make baking easy by letting you make batter yeast breads, quick breads, and cakes that take little time.

The eveness of heat provided by the natural stoneware is a plus for certain of these breads and cakes. Those highly sweetened or containing lots of fruit won't scorch as easily in crocks as in a metal pan. There's no need for lining pans with brown paper or covering with foil during baking, and baking temperatures can be higher with crocks than with conventional cookware. The stoneware makes breads and cakes you'd normally steam, like Christmas Plum Pudding, seem like you did, but with much less time and watching.

This chapter is full of holiday baking ideas. The baking crocks make breads which are a perfect "gift-giving" shape. While the recipes here are sized to fit two crocks, some of your favorite recipes may not fit. Here are some guidelines to help adapt your recipe:

For **yeast breads**, the rule of thumb is a recipe containing 4 cups of flour without a lot of other ingredients. If you have a kitchen scale, weigh the dough. A pound of dough is perfect for one crock. Or, fill the crock no more than two-thirds full. Let the dough rise to the top of the crock before baking.

For **quick breads and cakes**, measure the volume of the prepared batter in a standard glass liquid measure. A baking crock will hold two cups of batter. That amount fills the crock about two-thirds full, and allows room for the batter to rise during baking.

For **fruitcakes**, which tend to rise less than do breads and cakes, fill crocks three-quarters full, or with about two and a half cups of batter.

Many batters and quick breads are sized to the standard 9 x 5-inch loaf pan. The volume of batter in those recipes is generally too much for two crocks, but works for three crocks.

Other containers can be used to hold the remaining batter from a favorite recipe. Think of cupcakes! Midget loaf pans are helpful, as are soup cans from 16-ounce fruit and vegetable cans.

Use the recipes in this chapter as guides for baking times of yeast breads, quick breads, and cakes. Baking times are not a great deal shorter in baking crocks. Start checking about 15 to 20 minutes before normal baking time ends.

Test for doneness by inserting a cake tester into center of the bread or cake. If the tester comes out clean, the bread or cake is done. Make note of the baking time on the recipe so that you have a record of it for another time.

Baking Crock Yeast Breads

A number of the bread recipes in this chapter are for what's known as batter breads. Batter breads have coarser crumbs and a thicker, rougher crust because the dough isn't kneaded. Perfect for someone just starting, or someone with a limited amount of time, batter breads are also easily made with a heavy-duty mixer.

The steps in making batter breads differ somewhat from the breadmaking information given in the Superstone chapter because this "mixer method" is used. In this method, undissolved yeast, is mixed with some of the dry ingredients. Generally, these recipes use more yeast than is used in conventional breadmaking recipes. Liquid ingredients are heated to a warmer temperature (120° to 130°), then mixed with the dry ingredients and yeast with a mixer for three to five minutes. More flour is added to make a stiff batter, which is again mixed with a mixer. These two steps take the place of kneading in a regular yeast bread.

The batter is covered, and allowed to rise in the mixing bowl. Instead of punching down the raised batter, it is stirred down until it almost regains its original volume.

The dough is then divided between two buttered baking crocks, usually filling them a little more than half full. The dough is allowed to rise to the tops of the crocks before baking.

These loaves can be tested for doneness with a cake tester or by tapping to see if they sound hollow. With either batter or regular yeast breads baked in crocks, I sometimes remove them from the crocks to finish baking right on the oven rack. This lets the sides of the loaves get golden brown and crusty.

ENGLISH MUFFIN BREAD

Perfect for slicing as a base for Eggs Benedict and other savory dishes, English Muffin Bread baked in a crock makes good sense. Makes two loaves.

Scant 1 tbsp. (1 pkg.) active dry yeast
1 1/2 cups warm milk
1 tbsp. sugar
3 3/4—4 cups unbleached
   all-purpose flour
1 tsp. salt
2 tbsp. softened butter
1/4 tsp. baking soda
1 tbsp. warm water
Cornmeal

Dissolve yeast in warm milk and sugar; let it proof. Stir in 2 cups flour, salt, and butter, beat until smooth. Stir in enough of the remaining flour to make a stiff batter. Cover and let rise in a warm place until doubled in size, about 1 1/2 hours.

Dissolve baking soda in warm water. Stir down the batter and add dissolved baking soda, mixing until well blended. Divide batter and fill 2 baking crocks that have each been generously buttered and coated with about 2 tsp. of cornmeal. Sprinkle tops of batter with additional cornmeal. Cover and let rise until dough reaches tops of crocks, about 30 minutes. Bake on lower shelf in 350° oven for 30 to 35 minutes until light golden brown. Remove from crocks and, if desired, return to oven for a few minutes to give loaves additional color. Let loaves cool on a rack.

WHOLE GRAIN HERB BREAD

This herb-filled loaf is full of whole-grain goodness and has an almost steamed bread texture. You can use part all-purpose flour if you like a lighter texture. The sesame variation is one we like to toast. Makes two loaves.

Scant 2 tbsp. (2 pkgs.) active dry yeast
1 13-oz. can evaporated milk **or**
    1 1/2 cups light cream
    (room temperature)
2 tbsp. honey

About 4 cups stone-ground whole
    wheat or graham flour
3/4 cup stone-ground yellow cornmeal
2 tbsp. chopped fresh sage
1 tbsp. chopped fresh dill
1 tbsp. instant minced onion
3 tbsp. softened butter

Dissolve yeast in milk and honey. When proofed, mix in 1 cup flour and remaining ingredients; blend well. Stir in enough of the remaining flour to make a stiff dough or cover and let rest about 20 minutes. Turn out onto lightly floured board and knead until smooth, about 5 minutes. Place in a greased bowl and turn to coat the surface. Cover and let rise in a warm place until doubled in size, about an hour.

Punch down the dough. Divide dough into 2 equal portions. Form each into a rounded teardrop-shaped loaf and place in buttered baking crocks. Cover and let rise until dough reaches 1 inch above tops of crocks. Bake on lower shelf in 350° oven for 35 to 40 minutes until tops are golden brown and loaves sound hollow when tapped. Remove from crocks and, if desired, return to oven for a few minutes to give loaves additional color. Brush tops of loaves with a little melted butter and let cool on a rack.

For **Whole Grain Sesame Bread** omit herbs and onion. Use 1/2 cup sesame seed for 1/2 cup whole wheat flour.

CHEESY BEER BREAD

Toasted with garlic butter, this bread is a tasty complement to barbecued steaks or ribs. Makes two loaves.

1 1/2 cups (6 oz.) shredded American
  or colby cheese
1 tsp. salt
1 tbsp. sugar
1/2 cup beer
1/2 cup milk
2 tbsp. butter or margarine
2 1/2—3 cups unbleached all-purpose
  flour
Scant 1 tbsp. (1 pkg.) active dry yeast
1 egg

Heat cheese, salt, sugar, beer, milk and butter until very warm. Combine 1 cup flour and yeast. Add egg and cheese mixture to flour mixture. Blend at low speed, then beat 3 minutes at medium speed. With heavy-duty mixer or wooden spoon, stir in enough of the remaining flour to make a stiff batter. Cover and let rise in a warm place until light and doubled in size, about an hour.

Stir down the batter. Divide batter and fill 2 baking crocks that have been generously greased. Cover and let rise until dough reaches tops of crocks, about 45 minutes. Bake on lower shelf in 350° oven for 25 to 30 minutes until golden brown. Remove from crocks and, if desired, return to oven for a few minutes to give loaves added color. Brush warm loaves with softened butter. Let loaves cool on a rack.

DILL

DILL CHEESE BREAD

Everyone's favorite batter bread, the taste of dill and cheese makes this bread special. This version has been developed to perfectly fit the baking crocks. Makes two loaves.

1 cup ricotta, farmer's, or dry curd
  cottage cheese
1/2 cup warm water
2 tbsp. butter or margarine
2 1/2—3 cups unbleached
  all-purpose flour
1/4 cup wheat germ, seven-grain cereal
  or miller's bran
3 tbsp. sugar
Scant 2 tbsp. (2 pkgs.) active dry yeast
1 tbsp. instant minced onion
1 tbsp. finely chopped fresh dill or
  2 tsp. dill weed
1 tsp. salt
1/2 tsp. baking soda
1 egg

Heat cheese, water, and butter until very warm. Combine 1 cup flour, wheat germ, sugar, yeast, onion, dill, salt, and baking soda. Add egg and cheese mixture to flour mixture. Blend at low speed, then beat 3 minutes at medium speed. With heavy-duty mixer or wooden spoon, stir in enough of the remaining flour to make a stiff batter. Cover and let rise in a warm place until light and doubled in size, about 1 1/2 hours.

Stir down the batter. Divide batter and fill 2 baking crocks that have been generously greased. Cover and let rise until dough reaches tops of crocks, about 45 minutes. Bake on lower shelf in 350° oven for 35 to 40 minutes until golden brown. Remove from crocks and, if desired, return to oven for a few minutes to give loaves added color. Brush warm loaves with softened butter and if desired sprinkle with coarse salt. Let loaves cool on a rack.

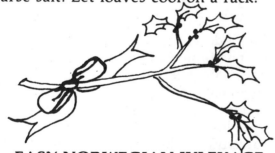

EASY NORWEGIAN JULEKAGE

These lovely frosted crowns are easily made for busy Christmas times because they're finished in just about two hours. Makes two loaves.

1 cup milk
1/4 cup butter
2 1/2—3 cups unbleached all-purpose flour
1/4 cup sugar
Scant 2 tbsp. (2 pkgs.) active dry yeast
1 tsp. salt
1 tsp. freshly ground cardamon
1 egg
1 cup chopped mixed candied fruit
1/2 cup light raisins

Egg glaze, page 20

Heat milk and butter until very warm. Combine 1 cup flour, sugar, yeast, salt and cardamon in large mixing bowl. Add egg and milk mixture to flour mixture. Beat until smooth, about 2 minutes. Stir in fruit and raisins. Gradually stir in remaining flour to make a stiff batter.

Either cover batter, and let rise until doubled, about 1 1/2 to 2 hours, or immediately divide batter and fill 2 generously greased baking crocks. If dough is allowed to rise in the bowl, stir down the batter, then fill crocks. Let dough rise in crocks until batter reaches the tops of the crocks. Brush with egg glaze. Bake on lower shelf of 350° oven for 25 to 30 minutes until dark golden brown. Remove from crocks, and let loaves cool on a rack. When cooled, frost with Brown Butter Icing, (page 58), and decorate with pearl sugar or additional candied fruit pieces.

APRICOT OATMEAL BREAD

Apricots and currants mingle in a tender sweetened dough and make this a moist bread that keeps well. We've taken it camping to eat for breakfast with eggs and sausage. Makes two loaves.

1 cup milk
1/2 cup rolled oats
1/2 cup dried apricots, cut in small
    pieces (about 10 halves)
1/4 cup currants
2 tbsp. cooking oil
2 tsp. salt
Scant 1 tbsp. (1 pkg.) active dry yeast
1/2 cup warm water
2 tbsp. sugar
1 egg
3 1/2—4 cups unbleached
    all-purpose flour

Melted butter
Cinnamon-sugar mixture

Heat the milk to scalding, and combine with the rolled oats, apricots, currants, cooking oil, and salt. Mix and let cool to lukewarm. In a large mixing bowl, dissolve yeast in warm water and sugar; let it proof.

Add oats mixture and egg to yeast mixture; blend well. Stir in 2 cups flour; beat until smooth. Stir in enough additional flour to form a soft dough. Turn out on lightly floured board and knead until smooth, adding flour as needed to prevent sticking. Place in a greased bowl and turn to

coat the surface. Cover and let rise in a warm place until doubled in size, about 1 1/2 hours.

Punch down the dough and divide into 2 equal portions. Form each into a rounded teardrop-shaped loaf, placing each in a greased baking crock. Cover and let rise until dough reaches the tops of the crocks. Bake on lower shelf in 375⁰ oven for 25 to 30 minutes until cake tester inserted in loaves comes out clean. Remove from the crocks and brush tops generously with melted butter. Sprinkle with a mixture of cinnamon and sugar. Let cool before storing or slicing.

RUSSIAN EASTER BREAD

A cake-textured coffee bread, this traditional **kulich** is usually baked to enormous proptions. In baking crock-size, it can be enjoyed anytime. Makes two loaves.

1/4 cup light raisins
1/4 cup dark rum or a Muscat-type wine
Scant 1 tbsp. (1 pkg.) active dry yeast
1/4 cup warm water
1/2 cup whipping cream (room temperature)
1/3 cup honey
1/4 cup softened butter
1 tsp. vanilla

3 eggs
3 1/2—4 cups unbleached all-purpose flour
1/2 tsp. salt
1/4 cup slivered blanched almonds, lightly toasted

Melted butter
Powdered sugar

Mix raisins with rum in a bowl and let stand while preparing sponge. Dissolve yeast in the water in a large mixing bowl, let it proof. Add cream, honey, butter, vanilla, and eggs, mixing well. Stir in 1 cup flour and salt, then beat until smooth. Cover and let rest in a warm place for about an hour, until mixture is bubbly and spongelike.

Stir the sponge down, adding raisins, almonds, and enough of the remaining flour to make a soft dough. Turn out on a floured board and knead a few times until dough is no longer sticky and is easy to handle. Knead until smooth and elastic, adding as little flour as necessary to make a soft, tender dough. Place in a greased bowl and turn to coat the surface. Cover and let rise in a warm place until doubled in size, about an hour.

Punch down the dough. Divide dough into 2 equal portions and form each into a rounded teardrop-shaped loaf, placing each in a buttered baking crock. Cover and let rise until dough reaches the tops of the crocks. Bake on lower shelf in 350° oven for 30 to 35 minutes until cake tester inserted in loaves comes out clean. Remove from crocks and brush tops of loaves with a little melted butter. While warm, either sprinkle with powdered sugar or drizzle with Brown Butter Icing, page 58, using rum for a little of the liquid.

Quick Breads And Cakes

Unlike slow rising yeast breads, quick breads and rich moist cakes become leavened as soon as the liquid ingredients are combined with baking powder or baking soda. These breads and doughs are mixed by first creaming sugar, shortening, and eggs. Then, the dry ingredients are added, including the leavening, along with whatever else the recipe contains. Mixed just until combined, the batters are poured into crocks to bake. The "whatever else" is what makes these recipes favorites, for they often contain fruits, nuts, and wonderful spices.

These breads and cakes have a close, tender texture, and are unusually moist. Many are better when made a day or so ahead of serving; this waiting also makes slicing easier.

To use these recipes in a number of serving situations, the following toppings may be helpful.

BROWN BUTTER ICING

2 tbsp. butter or margarine
1/2 cup powdered sugar
1—2 tbsp. light cream

Brown butter in small saucepan over medium heat. Add remaining ingredients; beat until smooth.

For **Butter Rum Icing**, use rum for part of the cream.

SAVORY CHEESE SPREAD

1 package (8 oz.) softened cream cheese
3 tbsp. steak sauce
2 tbsp. finely chopped onion
1/4 tsp. mustard

Combine all ingredients; mix well. A favorite with Walnut Prune Bread and other nut breads.

CORN SYRUP GLAZE

Brush cooled quick breads and fruit cakes with warm corn syrup. If desired, decorate with whole nuts or candied fruit.

BRANDY HARDSAUCE

1 cup powdered sugar
1/4 cup softened butter
1—2 tbsp. brandy or rum
1/2 tsp. vanilla

Combine all ingredients; mix until well blended. Chill before serving. A favorite with Applesauce Nut Cake or steamed puddings.

GOLDEN BUTTER SAUCE

1/4 cup butter
1/2 cup sugar
2 tbsp. cornstarch or 1 tbsp. arrowroot
1 1/2 cup water
1/4 cup orange juice or 2 tbsp.
   lemon juice

Melt butter over medium heat in 1-quart saucepan. Stir in sugar and cornstarch, add remaining ingredients. Cook, stirring occasionally, until sauce comes to a boil (about 5 minutes). Let boil 1 minute. A favorite with Pineapple Carrot Cake.

NATURALLY DELICIOUS FRUIT CAKE

This is my favorite kind of fruitcake made with natural fruits and lots of nuts. The mixture of fruits for this recipe comes from a health food store. If fruits seem dry, as naturally dried ones sometimes do, soak in fruit juice, sherry, or an orange-flavored liqueur. Drain well before adding to fruit-cake batter. For best results, bake three to four weeks before using. Makes two loaves.

3/4 cup unbleached all-purpose flour
3/4 cup sugar
1/2 tsp. baking powder
1 1/2 tsp. vanilla
3 eggs
4 cups (1 lb.) dried mixed fruit
   (such as apricots, pineapple, white and
   black figs, papaya and apples)
2 cups Muscat raisins
.2 cups (8 oz.) pecan halves

Combine flour, sugar, baking powder, vanilla, and eggs; mix well. Stir fruits and nuts into batter. Pour into 2 generously greased baking crocks, pressing down gently with a spoon so that crocks are filled evenly. Bake in 300° oven for 60 to 75 minutes until cake tester inserted in center comes out clean. (Cover crocks with foil for last half hour if browning seems excessive.) Cool in crocks on cooling rack for an hour. Run a narrow knife or spatula around edge of crock, remove cakes, and continue cooling. If desired, wrap cooled cakes in cheese cloth that has been dipped in sherry or orange-flavored liqueur. Place in plastic bag and refrigerate to ripen at least a week before slicing; several weeks is even better. If desired, glaze before serving.

CARIOCA CHOCOLATE BREAD

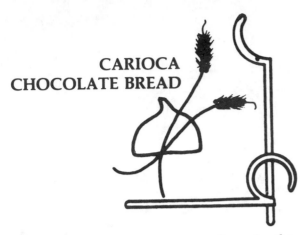

Potatoes are a surprise ingredient in this moist, brownie-like bread, so it's good to remember this recipe when there are leftovers. The chocolate, cinnamon, currant, and rum flavors are a winning combination. Makes two loaves.

- 1 cup sugar
- 2/3 cup cocoa
- 1/3 cup softened butter
- 3 eggs
- 1 cup mashed potatoes
- 1/3 cup milk
- 1 1/2 cups unbleached all-purpose flour
- 1 tbsp. baking powder
- 1 tsp. cinnamon
- 1/2 tsp. salt
- 1 cup currants
- 1 cup chopped nuts

Cream sugar, cocoa, and butter in a large mixing bowl. Beat in eggs one at a time. Stir in potatoes and milk, blending until smooth. Add flour, baking powder, cinnamon, and salt, stirring just until blended. Stir in currants and nuts.

Pour into 2 generously greased baking crocks. Bake in 350° oven for about 55 minutes until cake tester inserted in center comes out clean. Cool 10 minutes; remove from crocks and cool on a rack. When completely cool, place in plastic bag and let stand overnight before slicing. If desired, drizzle with Butter Rum Icing, page 58.

BANANA POUNDCAKE

Banana flavor in a firm textured poundcake is unbeatable. Try topping poundcake slices with vanilla ice cream, sliced banana, and a caramel pecan dessert sauce. Makes two loaves.

- 2/3 cup butter
- 1 cup sugar
- 3 eggs
- 2 cups unbleached all-purpose flour
- 3/4 tsp. baking powder
- 1/2 tsp. cinnamon
- 3/4 cup mashed ripe bananas (about 3 medium sized)
- 1 tsp. vanilla

Cream butter with sugar in mixing bowl. Add eggs; beat well. Add remaining ingredients and stir until combined.

Pour into 2 baking crocks that have been generously greased. Bake in 350° oven for 50 to 60 minutes until cake tester inserted in center comes out clean. Let cool 10 minutes before removing from crocks. If desired serve sprinkled with powdered sugar, or use slices as a base for fruit, pudding, or ice cream toppings.

WALNUT FRUIT BREAD

1 egg
1/4 cup brown sugar
1/2 cup honey
1/4 cup cooking oil
Grated peel of 1 orange (about 1 tbsp.)
Juice of 1 orange and milk to make 1 cup
1 cup stone-ground whole wheat or
    graham flour
1 cup unbleached all-purpose flour
2 tsp. baking powder
1/2 tsp. baking soda
1/2 tsp. salt
1 cup chopped walnuts
1/2 cup pitted prunes, dates, or figs,
    cut into small pieces

Beat egg with sugar, honey, cooking oil, and orange peel in mixing bowl. Stir in orange juice and milk. Add remaining ingredients except nuts and prunes; stir until combined. Stir in nuts and prunes.

Pour into 2 baking crocks that have been generously greased. Bake in 350° oven for 35 to 40 minutes until cake tester inserted in center comes out clean. Let cool 10 minutes before removing from crocks; let cool completely before slicing. Goes well with whipped cream cheese or Savory Cheese Spread, page 58.

APPLESAUCE NUT CAKE

Makes two loaves.

2 eggs
1 cup brown sugar
1/3 cup cooking oil
2 cups unbleached all-purpose flour
1 1/2 tsp. baking soda
1 tsp. cinnamon
1/2 tsp. salt
1/2 tsp. cloves
1 1/2 cups unsweetened applesauce
1 cup chopped nuts

Beat eggs, sugar, and oil in mixing bowl. Adding remaining ingredients except nuts and stir until combined. Stir in nuts.

Pour into 2 baking crocks that have been generously greased. Bake in 350° oven for 50 to 60 minutes until cake tester inserted in center comes out clean. Let cool 10 minutes before removing from crocks. Let cool completely before slicing or frosting.

PINEAPPLE CARROT CAKE

A nice variation to a classic cake! The Golden Butter Sauce, (page 59), makes this a company-perfect dessert. Makes two loaves.

2 eggs
1 cup sugar
3/4 cup cooking oil
2 tsp. vanilla
2 cups unbleached all-purpose flour
1 tsp. baking powder
1 tsp. baking soda

1 tsp. cinnamon
1/2 tsp. salt
1 cup finely shredded carrots
   (about 2 medium)
1 cup (8 oz. can) crushed pineapple
   with juice

Beat eggs with sugar, oil and vanilla in mixing bowl. Add remaining ingredients and stir until combined and all ingredients are moistened.

Pour into 2 baking crocks that have been generously greased. Bake in 350° oven for 50 to 60 minutes until cake tester inserted in center comes out clean. Let cool 10 minutes before removing from crocks. Let cool completely before slicing or frosting.

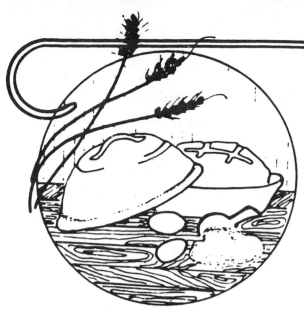

CHAPTER FOUR
LA CLOCHE

La Cloche is a brick oven in miniature. Comprised of two parts, the bottom portion is similar to a deep dish pizza/pie baker while the top is a domed cover with a handle.

Until the development of the iron kitchen range in the early 19th century, home baking in most of western and northern Europe, as well as in North America, was done in enclosed brick ovens. The oven bricks were heated with coals that were raked out before the loaves were inserted for baking. The oven door was then sealed into place, and in the slackening heat the week's baking was done. Breads were baked first, then cakes, pastries, or cobblers were baked in the lower residual heat.

While the iron kitchen range was a great advance in convenience and conservative use of fuel, particularly for city dwellers, it had recognized shortcomings. The system of flues and dampers needed to regulate the heat of a range created a much dryer oven heat than did the brick oven. Our modern gas and electric ovens are vast im-

provements over these early ovens, but they have the same shortcomings with regard to the dry heat generated.

Moist heat allows gases formed by yeasts to expand to greater volume in a dough before a crust forms. The character of the crust is chewy, with a remarkable blistered crustiness. Breads have a lighter, more open texture. These loaves, the goal of every home baker of traditional "honest" bread, are accomplished easily in La Cloche. There's no need to resort to all the techniques -- pans of boiling water, ice cubes tossed on the oven floor, or misting with water -- that used to be used to introduce moisture in the modern oven.

The other cooking technique possible with La Cloche is one that also has a long history. The use of soft clay or large leaves to wrap meats before roasting, thus preserving moisture and reducing shrinkage, dates to prehistoric times. La Cloche produces similar results with much less effort.

Clay cookers make good sense these days. As we choose meat cuts, poultry, and fish for their economy and lower proportions of fat, we need cooking techniques that insure moistness. La Cloche is one of a number of clay cookers that accomplish this task. Favorite recipes for meat dishes that are pot roasted or braised, or poultry and fish dishes that are baked or poached in covered pans, can be adapted to La Cloche.

The results of using La Cloche are unique, however the bread recipes in this chapter can certainly be made using Superstone tiles or baking stones. Baking directions are suggested with each recipe. If you use a baker other than La Cloche, follow methods and baking directions provided with your particular clay cooker or casserole.

"Undercover" Bread Baking

The bread recipes in this chapter are very basic, but are among the best in the book. Like any bread that contains little shortening, these are best either eaten as soon as possible after baking or frozen immediately to preserve freshness.

Many other breads bake beautifully in La Cloche, so use these recipes as guides to the techniques to use with your personal bread favorites. Substituting water for milk in a recipe helps give the crust added crispness. The index suggests bread recipes found in other sections of this book which are also good to try "undercover."

These recipes show two baking methods. The first recipe, Crusty Country Loaf, uses only one baking temperature. In the other two recipes, the Pueblo Indian Bread and the Irish Oatmeal Sourdough Bread, the oven temperature is lowered twice during baking. This latter method most authentically represents the slackening heat of the brick oven, but may require more watching than you care to do. Either method works fine for all of the recipes.

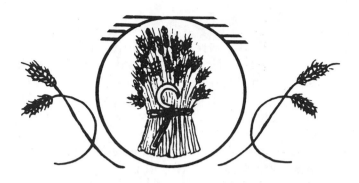

CRUSTY COUNTRY LOAF

Bread in the traditional country style, made with the simplest ingredients. My favorite flour for this loaf comes from a Missouri Mill and is a stoneground white flour with flecks of golden bran. Makes one loaf.

1 tsp. active dry yeast
1 3/4 cups warm water
About 5 cups unbleached all-purpose or
    bread flour
1 tbsp. salt

Dissolve yeast in warm water in a large mixing bowl. Add about 1 cup of the flour and the salt; beat well. Add enough additional flour to make a stiff dough. Turn out onto a lightly floured board and knead for about 10 minutes, adding flour as needed, until dough is smooth. (Dough for free-form loaves needs to be a little stiffer than for pan loaves.) Place in a greased bowl and turn to coat the surface. Cover and let rise in a warm place until doubled, about an hour.

Punch down the dough, and knead a few times. (If dough seems soft you can knead in a little more flour at this point.) Let rise a second time. Punch dough down again and knead as before. Shape into a round or oval loaf, being careful to tuck dough under tightly so the ball of dough is very round and plump. Place loaf on the bottom portion of La Cloche that has been buttered. Let dough rise, covered, while oven and La Cloche cover preheat to 425°, about 20 minutes. A few minutes before baking, gently plump the shaped loaf, and slash the top deeply with a sharp knife or scissors.

Place the preheated cover over the loaf, and place La Cloche in the oven. Bake for 30 minutes. Remove the cover and continue baking for 10 to 15 minutes, until loaf is desired crispness and golden brown color. Remove from pan onto a rack to cool. Makes 1 loaf.

For **Whole Grain Country Loaves**, use 1/2 cup whole wheat flour in place of 1/2 cup of the all-purpose flour. Or, add 2 tbsp. miller's bran or wheat germ.

PUEBLO INDIAN BREAD

Baked in a beehive-shaped adobe oven called a **hornos**, this Indian bread from the Southwest is honest American baking at its native best. Baking in the La Cloche will make a fairly authentic version that's shaped to represent the sun. Makes one loaf.

Scant 1 tbsp. (1 pkg.) active dry yeast
1/4 cup warm water
2 tbsp. lard or shortening, melted
   and cooled
1 tsp. salt
3 1/2—4 cups unbleached
   all-purpose flour
1 cup warm water

Dissolve yeast in 1/4 cup warm water in large mixing bowl. Stir in lard and salt. Add 3 cups flour alternately with the remaining water, beating after each addition. Turn out onto lightly floured board and knead, adding remaining flour as needed, until dough is smooth and elastic (about 8 to 10 minutes). Place in a greased bowl and turn to coat the surface. Cover and let rise in a warm place until doubled in size, about an hour. Punch down the dough, turn out on lightly floured board, and knead 2 to 3 more minutes. Cover and let rest 10 to 15 minutes.

To shape loaf, roll ball of dough into a 9-inch circle. Fold circle almost in half. (Top circular edge should be about 1 inch from bottom circular edge.) Place in bottom portion of La Cloche that has been buttered. With scissors, make about 4 cuts crosswise in the circular edge of the top half of the dough. Cover and let rise until almost doubled in size.

About 20 minutes before loaf is ready to bake, preheat the oven and La Cloche cover to 425°. Gently plump shaped loaf. Place the preheated cover over the loaf, and place La Cloche in the oven. Bake for 20 minutes. Remove the cover, reduce oven temperature to 400°, and continue baking 10 more minutes. Reduce oven temperature to 350° and bake about 20 minutes more until loaf is of desired crispness and golden brown in color. Place loaf onto a rack to cool.

SOURDOUGH IRISH OATMEAL BREAD

Irish oatmeal is not the rolled oats with which Americans are familiar but instead is like the steel cut oats available at food Co-ops. The baking of these loaves, one in La Cloche and one on a Superstone baking stone, sounds complicated. It's not, and can be done with only one oven by allowing the dough used for the La Cloche loaf to rise a second time, and by shaping it when the Superstone loaf is put into the oven to bake. Makes two loaves.

1 cup McCann's Irish Oatmeal
1 cup boiling water
1 tsp. yeast
1/4 cup water
2 tbsp. honey
2 cups sourdough starter batter
4—4 1/2 cups unbleached
   all-purpose flour
1 tsp. salt

Pour boiling water over oatmeal in a mixing bowl; let it cool to lukewarm, about 20 minutes. Combine yeast with the water and honey in a large mixing bowl; let it proof until foamy. Add sour dough batter, 2 cups flour, and the salt, mixing to form a stiff dough. Cover and let dough rest about 20 minutes. Turn out onto lightly floured board and knead, adding more flour as needed, until dough is smooth and elastic (about 10 minutes). Place dough in a greased bowl and turn to coat the surface. Cover and let rise in a warm place until doubled in size, about 1 1/2 hours. Dough may either be shaped at this point, or punched down to rise a second time. Shape into 2 free-form loaves, placing one loaf in the bottom portion of La Cloche that has been buttered, and allow the other to rise on a Superstone baking stone or cookie sheet that has been sprinkled with cornmeal. Cover and let rise until almost doubled in size.

Bake loaf on Superstone tile in a 400° oven for 25 to 30 minutes until golden brown.

About 20 minutes before loaf in La Cloche is ready to bake, heat the oven and La Cloche cover to 425°. Gently plump the shaped loaf, and slash the top with 6 cuts, making a criss-cross design. Place the preheated cover over the loaf, and place La Cloche in the oven. Bake for 20 minutes. Remove La Cloche cover, reduce oven temperature to 400°, and continue baking for 10 more minutes. Reduce oven temperature to 350° and bake about 20 more minutes until loaf is of desired crispness and golden brown in color. Remove from pan and place onto a rack to cool.

For **Cracked Wheat Sourdough Bread**, use 1 cup cracked wheat in place of Irish oatmeal.

Pot Roasting "Undercover"

The following cooking "undercover" ideas for meats, poultry, and fish are simple enhancements of quality ingredients which is the key to preparing country-style main dishes.

Roasting chicken or turkey in La Cloche is the easiest method I've found to preserve moistness while getting the flavor I prefer for sandwiches or salads.

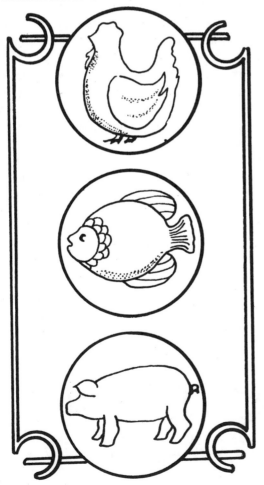

The fish recipes are simple and delicious. Whole fish can be used if you can find any that fit the baker! Stuffings are always a special treat. Try the one in the recipe for fillets of sole or a stuffing with herbs, tomato and onion slices.

You may want to line the bottom portion of La Cloche with heavy-duty foil when using these recipes.

Pot Roasts

Pot roasting beef "under clay" provides the moist heat needed to tenderize less tender cuts. Either chuck or rump roasts can be used, or sirloin tip, eye of the round, or heel of the round. Roasts either with or without the bone may be used. My preference is boneless rolled roast. It usually costs more per pound, but it roasts evenly and retains a good flavor.

Roasts that weigh about three pounds work well in La Cloche. To prepare the meat for roasting, first trim any excess fat from the roast. Then either marinate with roast marinade or brown the meat in a skillet, using oil or butter if needed.

Place the roast in the bottom portion of La Cloche that has been lined with heavy-duty foil. Season as desired with coarsely ground black pepper, herbs, or seasoned salt. Insert meat thermometer. Cover with La Cloche top and bake at 350° for 30 minutes . Reduce oven temperature to 300° and continue roasting for about an hour or until desired doneness.

Because the natural stoneware holds heat, it is a good idea to remove the roast from the oven when it is about 10 degrees from the doneness you desire. Covered with the La Cloche top, it should reach your desired doneness and be ready to carve in about 15 minutes.

To bake vegetables along with the roast, cut into 3/4-inch slices and add at the beginning of the cooking period. Potatoes, turnips, rutabagas, onions, and carrots are good additions.

When a sauce or gravy is desired, some liquid needs to be added to La Cloche. Brown stock, beef bouillon, water, the marinade, wine, or spirits can be used. About one cup will be needed. Sauce can be thickened with Beurre manies, and seasoned to taste. Sauteed fresh mushrooms can be added. For a richer colored sauce, add a little meat glaze coloring or Worcestershire sauce.

WINE MARINATED POT ROAST

Serves eight to ten.

3 lbs. boneless bottom round roast
  or other pot roast
1 cup dry red wine
1 tbsp. chopped fresh sage, thyme,
  parsley, or other favorite herb
1 tbsp. cooking oil
2 cloves garlic, minced
8—10 small onions, peeled and sliced
6—8 carrots, peeled and sliced diagonally
Coarsely ground black pepper
1 cup (1/2 pt.) small whole or quartered
  larger mushrooms
2 tbsps. butter
Beurre manie, made by combining 1 tbsp.
  flour with 1 tbsp. softened butter

Prepare meat for roasting. In glass or ceramic bowl, or in a large plastic bag, combine wine, sage, oil, and garlic to form marinade. Marinate beef for 2 to 3 hours at room temperature, or 12 to 24 hours in the refrigerator. Roast should stand at room temperature at least an hour before roasting. Place roast in bottom portion of La Cloche along with onions and carrots. Sprinkle meat with pepper. Add marinade to baker, and insert meat thermometer. Cover with La Cloche top and place baker in 350° oven for 30 minutes. Reduce oven temperature to 300° and continue roasting about another hour. Begin checking roast after 45 minutes; roast until almost desired doneness or until the meat is fork tender. Remove roast and vegetables from baker to warm platter, cover.

Saute mushrooms in butter until lightly browned. Pour pan juices into a saucepan and reduce sauce slightly, skimming off the fat. Thicken with Beurre manie, whisking it in bit by bit, until sauce is of desired consistency. Stir mushrooms into sauce. Taste, season, and add meat glaze coloring, as desired. Slice roast, then spoon some of the mushroom sauce over the meat. Serve the remaining sauce on the side.

BEER MARINATED POT ROAST

Serves eight to ten.

3 lbs. boneless pot roast
1 1/2 cups (12 oz. can) beer
2 tsp. chopped fresh thyme or other
   favorite herb
2 medium onions, chopped
2 medium rutabagas, peeled and cut into
   1/2-inch slices (about 2 1/2 lbs.)
4—6 carrots, cut into lengthwise slices

Prepare meat for roasting. In glass or ceramic bowl, or in a large plastic bag, combine beer, thyme, and onions for marinade. Marinate beef 2 to 3 hours at room temperature, or 12 to 24 hours in the refrigerator. Roast should stand at room temperature at least an hour before roasting. Place roast in bottom portion of La Cloche along with rutabagas and carrots. Add marinade to baker. Insert meat thermometer. Cover with La Cloche top and place baker in 350° oven for 30 minutes. Reduce oven temperature to 300° and continue roasting about another hour. Begin checking roast after 45 minutes; roast until almost desired doneness or until meat is fork tender. Remove roast from baker to a warm platter, cover. Rutabagas and carrots can be served as they are, or mashed with 1 to 2 tbsp. butter and a little of the cooking liquid, if needed. Thicken broth, if desired, and serve on the side.

GLAZED CORNED BEEF WITH CARROTS AND PRUNES

Try this with mixed dried fruits if you are not fond of prunes. In either case, it's a flavorful combination. Makes four to six servings.

3—4 lb. corned beef brisket
4 large carrots, pared and cut in
   bias-cut slices (about 1 lb.)
1 cup pitted prunes
1 orange, sliced
1 medium onion, sliced
2 tbsp. fresh savory,
   tarragon, or other herb

Honey-orange glaze, below

Trim any excess fat from brisket. Cover brisket with water, let soak 1 hour, then rinse and pat dry. Arrange brisket in bottom portion of La Cloche along with carrots, prunes, orange, and onion. Sprinkle with savory. Cover and put in 325° oven for about 3 hours or until tender. Remove cover, brush with Honey-orange glaze, and return to oven for 10 to 15 minutes, just until glaze is bubbly. Watch carefully so that fruits and vegetables do not dry out.

To make **Honey-orange glaze**, combine 2 tbsp. each brown sugar and honey, and 1 tbsp. orange juice; blend well.

NEW ENGLAND STYLE CORNED BEEF

Oven roasting this traditional winter time favorite provides a hearty meal in one dish, with little effort for the cook. Serve with horseradish mustard and a favorite bread, such as the Dill Cheese Bread, page 54. Makes six servings.

2 1/2—3 lb. corned beef brisket
3 large potatoes, peeled and quartered lengthwise
6 medium carrots, peeled and cut in half crosswise
6 small onions, peeled
1 small head cabbage, cut into 6 wedges (about 1 lb.)

Trim any excess fat from brisket; pat dry. Arrange brisket in bottom portion of La Cloche along with potatoes, carrots and onions. Sprinkle with seasoning packet of herbs and spices. (If brisket does not come with seasonings, use 2 tsp. pickling spice or 1 bay leaf, 6 whole cloves, and 4 whole peppercorns.)

Cover with La Cloche top and put in 325° oven for 2 hours. Add cabbage wedges and continue baking, covered, an additional 30 minutes or until cabbage and corned beef are tender.

HERBED LAMB SHANK DINNER

Slow roasting is essential for lamb shanks, and roasting "undercover" with herbs and vegetables is a deliciously easy method of preparation. Makes four servings.

4 lamb shanks (about 2 1/2—3 lbs.)
2 tbsp. cooking oil
3 large carrots, pared and cut in lengthwise slices (about 1 lb.)
8 small onions, peeled
2 large potatoes, peeled and quartered lengthwise
1—2 tbsp. chopped fresh marjoram, rosemary, or other fresh herb
Salt and pepper
1/2 cup water

Trim any excess fat from lamb shanks, and brown them in oil in a large skillet. Arrange lamb shanks in bottom portion of La Cloche along with carrots, onions, and potatoes. Sprinkle with marjoram. Salt and pepper to taste. Add the water. Cover and put in 400° oven for 35 minutes. Reduce heat to 250° and continue to cook for 2—2 1/2 hours or until lamb shanks are tender.

PORK CHOPS WITH SWEET POTATOES AND APPLES

The natural sweetness of apples, dried apricots, and sweet potatoes is a perfect addition to pork. These pork chops are a good choice for fall menus because it is then that sweet potatoes and apples are at their freshest. Makes four servings.

4 pork chops
2—3 tbsp. butter and/or cooking oil
Salt and pepper
2 medium sweet potatoes or yams, peeled and cut in 1/4-in. slices
2 medium tart apples, peeled and quartered
1/2 cup (about 3 oz.) dried apricot halves
1/2—3/4 cup apple juice, cider, or apricot nectar
2 tbsp. honey
1/2 tsp. allspice or 1/4 tsp.
   each cinnamon and nutmeg
2 tbsp. melted butter

Trim excess fat from chops. Brown chops on both sides in butter in a large skillet over medium heat; season with salt and pepper. Arrange chops in bottom portion of La Cloche along with sweet potatoes, apples and apricots. Drain excess fat from skillet. Add apple juice, honey, and allspice to skillet and heat, stirring to loosen pan juices. Pour juice mixture over chops. Drizzle melted butter over sweet potatoes and fruits.

Cover with La Cloche top and place baker in 350° oven for about 1 hour or until chops are tender. Arrange chops, sweet potatoes, and fruits on warm serving platter; cover with La Cloche top. In small saucepan, combine 1 tsp. cornstarch with 1 tbsp. water; add pan juices and cook until mixture boils and thickens. Pour over chops, sweet potatoes, and fruits.

Poultry "Undercover"

Roasting chickens, small turkeys, or turkey breasts are easily cooked "under cover." The size birds used in the following recipes are best for La Cloche. Frozen poultry should be thawed before using. (A six to seven pound turkey breast takes about two days to thaw in the refrigerator.)

To prepare poultry for roasting, first remove giblets or seasonings, if present. Trim or pull away any excess fat from the bird. Rinse the bird inside and out; pat dry with paper towels. Place the stuffed or unstuffed bird in the bottom portion of La Cloche (lined with heavy-duty foil, if desired). Season to taste with salt, pepper, herbs, or garlic. Cover with La Cloche top and bake at 400° for one to two hours. If desired, take off La Cloche top when bird is almost done and continue to roast for 15 to 30 minutes. This allows the skin of the bird to brown. It is at this point that the bird may be glazed. Stuffed birds take slightly longer to roast than unstuffed birds.

Here are some hints for checking when poultry is done: a meat thermometer reading; a drumstick that moves easily up and down; or juices that do not run pink when the bird is pricked with a fork. Poultry will carve easier if it is allowed to set 10 to 15 minutes before slicing. Covered with La Cloche top, slightly ajar, the bird will remain warm. Covered completely, the bird may continue to roast because the natural stoneware cools slowly.

ORANGE BAKED CHICKEN

Leftovers of this orange-flavored bird make a delicious chicken salad. A touch of curry and chutney in the dressing is all that's needed for a special salad treat. Makes five to six servings.

3 1/2—4 lb. roasting chicken
1 orange, cut into 6 pieces
Salt and white pepper
1 1/2 cups apricot nectar
1/2 can (6 oz. size) frozen orange
    juice concentrate
1/2 cup light raisins
1 tbsp. chopped fresh sage,
    tarragon, or other herb
1/2 cup (4 oz. can) drained
    sliced mushrooms
Beurre manie, made by combining
    1 tbsp. flour with 1 tbsp.
    softened butter

Trim or pull away any excess fat from chicken. Fill cavity with orange sections. Truss the chicken and place in bottom portion of La Cloche. Salt and pepper. Combine apricot nectar, orange juice, raisins, and sage; add to baker. Cover and put in 400° oven for 1 hour. Uncover and continue to cook for 20 to 30 minutes, until chicken is browned and done. Remove chicken from baker and set aside to rest a few minutes before slicing.

Pour pan juices into a saucepan. Heat and reduce sauce slightly, skimming off the fat. Add mushrooms. Thicken with Beurre manie, whisking it in bit by bit, until sauce is of desired consistency. Serve over sliced chicken.

LA CLOCHE ROASTED TURKEY BREAST

Serve with a raisin-nut stuffing or with curry-seasoned rice. Serves twelve to fourteen.

6—7 lb. turkey breast
Seasoned salt and pepper
2 cloves garlic
6—8 sage leaves or other fresh herbs

Prepare turkey breast for roasting and place in bottom portion of La Cloche. Season with salt and pepper. Loosen skin enough on either side of breast so that garlic cloves can be placed between skin and breast meat. Insert garlic and add sage. Cover with La Cloche top and bake in a 400° oven for 1 1/2 hours. Uncover and glaze, if desired. Continue cooking for 15 to 30 minutes until bird is browned and done. Set aside to rest a few minutes before slicing.

For **Golden Oriental Glaze**, combine 1/3 cup soy sauce, 1/4 cup corn syrup, 2 tbsp. cooking oil, and 1 clove garlic, minced, or 1/4 tsp. garlic powder. Brush turkey with sauce.

For **Tarragon Lemon Glaze**, combine 1/4 cup lemon juice, 2 tbsp. cooking oil, 1 tbsp. chopped fresh tarragon, and 1/2 tsp. **each** paprika and seasoned salt. Brush turkey with sauce.

For **Barbecue Glaze**, combine 1/2 cup catsup, 1/4 cup honey, 2 tbsp. **each** cooking oil and vinegar, and 1/2 tsp. **each** ground cloves and seasoned salt. Brush turkey with sauce.

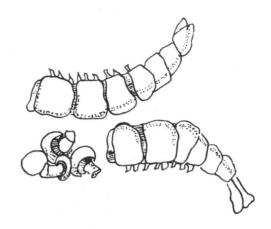

HALIBUT STEAKS WITH MUSHROOMS AND SHRIMP

A simple baked fish topped with a trio of favorite accompaniments: mushrooms, shallots, and shrimp. Try this recipe using snapper or swordfish steaks. Makes four servings.

2 halibut steaks (about 1 1/2 lbs.)
Lemon juice
2 tbsp. brandy
1 cup (1/2 pt.) sliced fresh mushrooms
2 medium shallots, finely minced (about 1/4 cup)
3 tbsp. butter
1 cup small cooked shrimp, thawed and drained
1 tbsp. snipped chives or chopped parsley

Rinse steaks in cold water and pat dry with paper towels. Brush both sides of steaks with lemon juice. Arrange in bottom portion of La Cloche and sprinkle with brandy.

Saute mushrooms and shallots in butter until soft and golden. Top steaks with shrimp and chives, then add mushroom mixture. Cover with La Cloche top and place in 400° oven for 15 to 20 minutes, or until fish flakes easily.

FILLETS OF SOLE WITH MUSHROOM STUFFING

Fish fit for company that cooks in 20 minutes is a pleasant surprise. The cream-enhanced pan juices add just a hint of richness to the finished fillets. Makes four servings.

2—4 fillets of sole (about 1 1/2 lbs.)
Lemon juice
1 egg
1 1/2 cup soft bread crumbs
1/2 cup (4 oz. jar) drained
   sliced mushrooms
2 tbsp. melted butter
2 tbsp. lemon juice
1 tbsp. chopped fresh parsley
Melted butter
1/4 cup dry white wine
1/2 cup heavy cream

Rinse fillets in cold water and pat dry with paper towels. Brush both sides of fillets with lemon juice.

To make stuffing, beat egg in medium bowl. Stir in bread crumbs, mushrooms, butter, lemon juice, and parsley until well blended. Using dark side of fillet as the inside, spoon stuffing onto half of each fillet, dividing evenly. Fold other half of fillet over stuffing. Arrange stuffed fillets in bottom portion of La Cloche. Brush fillets lightly with melted butter. Pour in wine.

Cover with La Cloche top and place in a 400° oven for 20 to 25 minutes, or until fish flakes easily. Arrange baked fillets on warm serving platter and cover with La Cloche top. Pour pan juices into saucepan, add cream, and boil hard until mixture coats a spoon. Taste and correct seasoning. Spoon sauce over fillets and, if desired, sprinkle with chopped parsley and lemon juice.

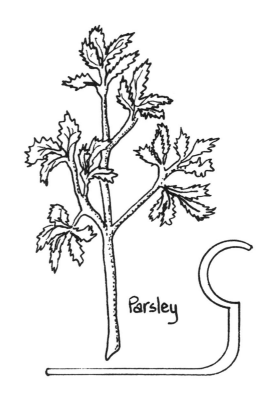
Parsley

CHAPTER FIVE
SUPERSTONE® DEEP DISH PIZZA/PIE BAKER

Pies for dessert are the hearty end to a simple country meal. Pies as a main dish are a meal in themselves. Bringing either of these kinds of pies to the table in a deep dish pizza/pie baker is a sight to behold. Pie pans aren't usually this attractive. The Superstone Deep Dish Pizza/Pie Baker is a natural for casual country dishes.

Deep dish pie fillings must bake slowly and thoroughly in order to thicken. A problem often arises when the crust, rich with shortening or butter, begins to darken and burn long before the filling bubbles or sets. The even heat distribution of Superstone pie bakers keeps this problem to a minimum. Pies can bake with little watching.

Yeast dough crusts benefit from the deep dish stoneware bakers in the same way crusts benefit from being baked on Superstone tiles. Deep dish pizzas have nicely browned crusts without being dry or tough. Sweetened yeast doughs in coffeecakes have similar results. Tamale pies, with their cooked cornmeal crusts, also benefit from the natural stoneware's even heating.

The size of the Superstone Deep Dish Pizza/Pie Baker makes it a perfect baking pan for family-size portions. Larger in diameter and deeper than standard pie pans, it most closely resembles a 10-inch deep dish pie pan or a shallow 1 1/2 quart casserole.

This chapter contains basic information on pastry and pie crusts. Because of the Superstone baker's size, and because it's made of unglazed stoneware, some adaptations to traditional recipes have been made.

Pies And Pastries

"Pies — wonderful pies" is a phrase often used to describe the memories of baking from our country kitchen. Cream pies topped with a cloud of gently swirled meringue are my mother's speciality. I learned early, however, that what separated one fine country baker from another was not the filling, but the quality of the flaky golden crusts of the best pies.

For most bakers pastry skill comes with lots of trial and error. Another of those simple mixtures like the best French bread, pastry contains little more than flour, shortening in some form, salt, and water. The key is to work quickly and to develop a light touch with the dough.

CLASSIC TART PASTRY

This pastry contains both butter and cooking oil, and is used for quiches and pies that have savory fillings. Combining oil and butter is a French technique that assures a light and tender crust.

2 cups unbleached all-purpose flour
Pinch of salt
1/2 cup chilled butter, cut into
　　small pieces
1 egg
4 tbsp. (1/4 cup) water
1 tbsp. cooking oil

Stir flour and salt together; cut in butter until mixture has the texture of coarse cornmeal. Beat the egg with the water and cooking oil. Add the egg mixture to the flour mixture while tossing with a fork. Use your hands to shape into a ball. Wrap in plastic wrap and refrigerate at least half an hour before using.

For **Whole Wheat Pastry**, use 1 cup whole wheat pastry flour for 1 cup all-purpose flour. Dough will be a little harder to roll out and shape than regular pastry.

For **Parmesan-Cornmeal Pastry**, use 1/2 cup stone-ground yellow cornmeal for 1/2 cup all-purpose flour, and add 2 tbsp. freshly grated Parmesan cheese. Dough may seem sticky at first, but moisture will be absorbed while the dough refrigerates.

STREUSEL TOPPING

Streusel toppings are the easy top crusts for fresh fruit pies. When using these on your favorite recipes, use less sugar in the filling.

3/4 cup all-purpose flour
1/2 cup brown sugar
1/2 tsp. nutmeg
1/3 cup butter

Combine flour, brown sugar, and nutmeg in a mixing bowl. Cut in butter until mixture is crumbly. Sprinkle over fruit filling or coffee cake.

RICH TART PASTRY

A slightly sweetened pastry to use with fresh fruit pies, this version of classic French pastry can be used in the Pie Baker without the usual pre-baking of the pastry shell.

1 1/2 cups unbleached all-purpose flour
1 tbsp. sugar
1/2 cup plus 2 tbsp. softened butter
4—6 tbsp. ice water

Stir together flour and sugar; cut in butter until pieces are the size of small peas. Gradually add the water while tossing dough with a fork until mixture clears the side of the bowl. Gently press together to form a ball. Refrigerate, wrapped in plastic wrap, for at least 1/2 hour.

SOUR CREAM TART PASTRY

Sour cream provides both the shortening and the liquid in this rich pastry that can be rolled out easily without first being refrigerated. Use this pastry anytime you use sour cream in pie filling.

3/4 cup butter
2 cups unbleached all-purpose flour
3 tbsp. sour cream

Cut butter into the flour until pieces resemble coarse cornmeal. Add the sour cream, tossing the mixture with a fork until it clears the side of the bowl. Gently press together to form a ball.

FLAKY "NEVER FAIL" PASTRY

Vinegar pastry is known for flakiness, and is one that's easy for a novice to handle in rolling and shaping. You need three cups of flour to make a double crust pie this size.

3 cups unbleached all-purpose flour
1 tsp. salt
1 cup shortening
1 egg
5 tbsp. ice water
1 tsp. vinegar

Stir together flour and salt; cut in shortening until mixture resembles coarse cornmeal. Beat the egg with the ice water and vinegar. Add the egg mixture to the flour mixture while tossing with a fork until mixture clears the side of the bowl. Gently press together to form a ball.

Steps In Making Pie And Pastry Crusts

Cut in butter (or shortening) until mixture resembles cornmeal. A pastry blender, or two knives, are used in this step to combine the shortening with the dry ingredients. Some food writers suggest using your fingers to blend the butter and flour. I like to use a food processor for this step, and have given directions for using one later in this section.

Gradually add water while tossing with a fork. This important step makes sure that the liquid is evenly distributed without too much mixing. The mixture will cling together at this point, and can be formed into a ball.

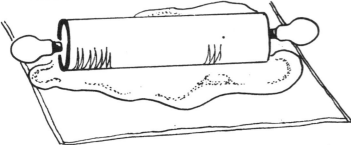

Transfer to deep dish pan. Getting the rolled pastry to the pan can be accomplished by gently rolling it onto the rolling pin, then gently easing it into place. The key to a pastry shell that doesn't shrink in baking is to not stretch it at this point.

Turn edges of dough under . . . After the dough is fitted into the pan, trim it so that only about an inch overhangs the edge. (For double crust pies, more can be trimmed off.) Turn this edge under to form a rim either by shaping it even with the edge of the pan or by pinching it to form a high, decorative, fluted edge.

On floured surface, roll pastry . . . The cooler the rolling surface, the better. That's why professionals use marble. A laminated counter top works better than a pastry board. I prefer a cloth-covered surface and a stockinette-covered rolling pin, because you use less flour when rolling the dough.

Shape the ball of dough into a flattened circle with smooth edges before rolling. This helps achieve the round circle you desire and prevents cracked, broken edges. If refrigerated doughs seem too stiff, let them stand a few minutes at room temperature. If dough seems soft, put it in the refreigerator or freezer for a few minutes.

For baked pastry shells from rich tart pastry doughs. Fit bottom of shaped pastry with a piece of waxed paper or foil and weight it down with about 2 cups of uncooked rice or beans (or cover with a layer of baker's pie weights). Bake in 375° oven for 15 minutes. Remove rice and paper. (Save and reuse the rice another time.) If pastry shell will be used without further baking, continue baking shell for 5 more minutes or until golden brown.

Brushing the top pastry of a double crust pie with milk and sprinkling with sugar makes an attractive finishing touch.

To ease pouring the egg mixture into a prepared quiche, first place the quiche on the extended rack of the oven. Pour egg mixture over the surface. Sprinkle with any remaining spices or cheese, then gently push the oven rack back into place.

Some Additional Hints

To use a food processor: Combine flour and other dry ingredients with **cold** butter, which has been cut into five or six pieces, in food processor bowl fitted with metal blade. Process until mixture resembles coarse cornmeal. If appropriate, add sour cream at this point. Combine liquid ingredients, if necessary. With machine running, add liquid ingredients through feed tube. Process just until dough begins to mass together to form a ball. Continue as directed in recipe.

Leftover pastry from any of the recipes keeps a few days in the refrigerator or can be frozen. The "leftovers" are great for shaping and baking in small individual quiches. Slip the baked shells out of the pans before freezing.

STREUSEL APPLE CAKE

This egg-rich yeast coffee cake is quickly mixed, and needs just one rise. Four variations give lots of choices! Serves eight.

Scant 1 tbsp. (1 pkg.) active dry yeast
1/2 cup warm milk (about 110°)
1/2 cup sugar
1/3 cup softened butter
2 tsp. grated lemon peel
2 eggs
2 cups unbleached all-purpose flour
1/2 tsp. salt
3 (3 cups) apples, peeled, cored,
   and sliced

Streusel Topping, below

Dissolve yeast in the warm milk in a large mixing bowl. Let stand until foamy and proofed, about 5 minutes. Meanwhile, cream sugar, butter, and lemon peel. Add eggs and beat until fluffy. Blend in dissolved yeast. Stir in flour and salt; beat until smooth.

Spread evenly in buttered deep dish pan. Arrange apple slices over batter in concentric circles. Sprinkle with Streusel Topping. Cover, and let rise in a warm place until doubled in size, about one hour. Bake in a 350° oven for 35 to 45 minutes until cake tester inserted in center comes out clean. If desired, dust with powdered sugar. Slice into wedges and serve hot.

For **Streusel Topping,** combine 1/3 cup all-purpose flour, 1/4 cup sugar, 1/2 tsp. cinnamon, and 3 tbsp. softened butter; mix until crumbly.

For **Streusel Plum Cake,** use about 1 1/2 lbs. (3 cups) small purple or red plums, pitted and quartered, in place of the apples.

For **Streusel Peach Cake,** use 3 large peaches, peeled, pitted, and sliced, in place of the apples. Double the amount of Streusel Topping.

For **Pecan Streusel Coffeecake,** reserve 1 egg yolk when making the dough. Omit the apples. Double the Streusel ingredients and, when combining, blend the egg yolk with the other ingredients; stir in 1/2 cup chopped pecans or other nuts.

CREAMY PEACH DEEP DISH PIE

This is a favorite pie that is not too sweet, and the crust and streusel steps are combined to save time. Makes eight servings.

Sour Cream Tart Pastry, page 81*

1/3 cup brown sugar
1/8 tsp. ginger
1 cup sour cream
1 egg
3 large (3 cups) fresh ripe peaches, peeled, pitted, and thickly sliced

Streusel topping, below

On floured surface, roll pastry into a 14-inch circle. Transfer to deep dish pan. Turn edges of dough under, pinching to form a high fluted edge. Prick pastry with a fork. Bake. Let cool about 20 minutes before adding filling.

Meanwhile, combine sugar, ginger, sour cream, and egg. Pour half the sour cream filling over the baked crust. Arrange the peach slices on top in concentric circles. Pour remaining filling over peaches, and sprinkle with streusel topping. Bake in a 400° oven for 25 to 30 minutes until topping is golden brown and filling is bubbly.

*Prepare **Sour Cream Tart Pastry** using 2 1/2 cups flour and 1 cup butter. Before adding sour cream, take out 1 cup of the mixture and set aside for Streusel Topping. Continue with recipe.

For **Streusel topping,** combine reserved pastry mixture with 1/4 cup brown sugar and 1/8 tsp. ginger.

PEAR MINCE PIE

Pears topped with mincemeat in a winter pie that's sure to please people who like mincemeat's spicy taste. Makes eight servings.

Flaky "Never Fail" Pastry, page 81

5 large (4 cups) fresh firm pears, peeled, cored, and sliced
1/2 cup sugar
2 tbsp. flour
2 cups prepared mincemeat

Milk
Sugar

On floured surface, roll out half of the pastry into a 14-inch circle. Transfer to a deep dish pan. Trim pastry even with the edge of pan.

Combine pears with sugar and flour. Fill pastry shell with pears; top pears with mincemeat.

On floured surface, roll out remaining pastry; cut slits for steam to escape. Moisten rim of bottom crust with water. Place top crust over filling. Trim edge 1/2 inch larger than bottom crust, and fold top edge under, pressing to seal. Flute edge. Brush top with milk and sprinkle with sugar. Baked in a 425° oven for 35 to 40 minutes until golden brown and filling is bubbly.

STREUSEL-TOPPED
PEACH BLUEBERRY PIE

These streusel-topped beauties are what a country deep dish pie should be. Fresh fruits make these farm stand specialties a delight as you can combine whatever fruits are in season. Makes eight servings.

Rich Tart Pastry, page 81

4 large (4 cups) fresh ripe peaches, peeled, pitted and sliced
2 cups fresh blueberries
1/2 cup brown sugar
2 tbsp. flour
1/2 tsp. nutmeg
1/4 tsp. ginger
2 tbsp. lemon juice

Streusel topping, page 83

On floured surface, roll pastry to a 14-inch circle. Transfer to deep dish pan. Turn edges of dough under, pinching to form high fluted edge.

Combine peaches and blueberries with sugar, flour, nutmeg, ginger, and lemon juice. Fill pastry shell with fruit mixture. Top fruit filling with streusel topping. Bake in a 425° oven for 45 to 50 minutes, until juice in center of pie is bubbly.

For **Streusel-Topped Melba Pie**, use fresh raspberries instead of blueberries.

CHOCOLATE PECAN PIE

Arranging pecan slices in a neat pattern, rounded sides up, in the bottom of the pie shell was one of my first ways of helping with the holiday pie baking. The chocolate

pie shown here is more like a rich pecan brownie than a pie. The Favorite Pecan Pie variation, a family tradition at Thanksgiving and Christmas, is the real thing! Makes eight servings.

Flaky "Never Fail" Pastry, page 81

3 (1 oz.) squares unsweetened chocolate
1/2 cup butter
4 eggs
1/2 cup brown sugar
1 cup light corn syrup
1 1/2 tsp. vanilla
1 1/2 to 2 cups pecan halves

On floured surface, roll out half the pastry into a 14-inch circle. Transfer to deep dish pan. Turn edges of dough under, pinching to form a fluted edge.

Melt chocolate with butter, allow to cool slightly. Beat eggs with sugar, then add corn syrup, vanilla, and the chocolate mixture. Beat until well blended. Stir in pecans and pour into pastry shell. Bake in a 350° oven for 35 to 40 minutes until center is set and puffy. Let cool on a rack. The pie will sink while it cools.

For **Chocolate Chip Pecan Pie**, use 1/2 to 1 cup semi-sweet chocolate chips for the chocolate squares. There's no need to melt the chips, just stir them into the filling with the pecans.

For **Favorite Pecan Pie**, omit the chocolate from this recipe. Use dark corn syrup for light corn syrup.

DUTCH CHEESE APPLE PIE

Apples and cheese — a winning combination in a pie that is traditionally what people mean when they say "deep dish pie." Makes eight servings.

Cheese Pastry, below

7 cups (7 medium) peeled, sliced
    apples (about 2 1/2 lbs.)
1/2 cup sugar
1 tsp. cinnamon

Streusel topping, page 83
1/2 cup shredded cheddar-type
    cheese

For **Cheese Pastry**, stir together 1 1/2 cups unbleached all-purpose flour and 1 cup shredded cheddar-type cheese; cut in 1/2 cup shortening until mixture resembles cornmeal. Gradually add 3 tbsp. water, tossing with a fork until mixture clears side of bowl. Gently press together to form a ball.

On floured surface, roll pastry into a 14-inch circle. Transfer to deep dish pan. Turn edges of dough under, pinching to form high fluted edge.

Combine apples with sugar and cinnamon. Fill pastry shell. Top fruit filling with Streusel topping. (To make topping for this pie, use cinnamon for nutmeg, and add shredded cheese with the flour.) Bake in a 375° oven for 45 to 50 minutes until juice in the center of pie is bubbly.

QUICHE LORRAINE

I had my first taste of quiche at Neiman-Marcus in Dallas when it came as my "potluck" luncheon entree. What an introduction! This version of that first classic is still my favorite. Makes six to eight servings.

Classic Tart Pastry, page 80

1 medium onion, thinly sliced
2 tbsp. butter
6 slices crisply cooked bacon,
    crumbled
1 cup thinly sliced ham,
    shredded (about 1/4 lbs.)
1 cup (4 oz.) shredded Swiss or
    gruyere cheese
4 eggs
1 1/2 cups light cream
    (half and half)
1/2 tsp. Dijon-style mustard
Nutmeg

On floured surface, roll pastry into a 14-inch circle. Transfer to deep dish pan. Turn edges of dough under, trimming if needed, shaping so that edge is flush with rim of pan. Prick bottom and sides with a fork. Bake at 375° for 15 minutes, following directions on page 82 for baked pastry shells. Let cool about 20 minutes before filling.

Saute onion in butter until soft. Sprinkle onion and bacon over bottom of prepared pastry. Add half of the ham and half of the cheese, then repeat layers using remaining ham and cheese. Beat eggs with the cream and mustard until thoroughly mixed.

Pour egg mixture over surface of prepared quiche. Sprinkle with nutmeg. Bake at 375° for 35 to 40 minutes until center is just set. (Custard will continue to set as it cools.) Cool on a rack for 10 minutes before cutting into wedges to serve.

For **Swiss Cheese Pie**, omit ham and bacon, and increase cheese to 2 cups (8 oz.).

SAVORY ONION QUICHE

Makes six to eight servings.

Sour Cream Tart Pastry, page 81, or Classic Tart Pastry, page 80

2 large onions, thinly sliced
1/4 cup butter
1 tbsp. chopped fresh oregano
1/2 tsp. salt

Dash of cayenne pepper
1 cup (4 oz.) shredded Swiss cheese
3 eggs
1 1/2 cups light cream **or** 3/4 cup light cream and 3/4 cup sour cream (or plain yogurt)

On floured surface, roll pastry into a 14-inch circle. Transfer to deep dish pan. Turn edges of dough under, trimming if needed, shaping so that edge is flush with rim of pan. Prick bottom and sides with a fork. Bake at 375° for 15 minutes, following directions on page 82 for baked pastry shell. Let cool about 20 minutes before filling.

Saute onions in butter until soft and golden. Add oregano, salt, and cayenne pepper. Spoon onions into prepared pastry, and sprinkle top with shredded cheese. Beat the eggs with the cream until thoroughly mixed.

Pour egg mixture over surface of prepared quiche. Bake at 375° for 35 to 40 minutes until center is just set. Cool on a rack about 10 minutes before serving.

For **Savory Onion-Tomato Quiche**, omit oregano in seasoning onions. Toss Swiss cheese with 2 tbsp. flour. When assembling quiche, sprinkle with only half of the cheese, then arrange slices of a large "meaty" tomato in a circular pattern on top. Sprinkle tomatoes with 1 tbsp. chopped fresh basil and the remaining cheese. Continue with recipe as directed.

CHEDDAR BROCCOLI QUICHE

Makes six to eight servings.

Classic Tart Pastry or any
  variation, page 80

1 small bunch (4 cups) broccoli, cut
  into 3/4-inch pieces
Salt
Few drops lemon juice
2 to 3 tbsp. Dijon-style mustard
2 cups (8 oz.) shredded
  cheddar cheese
4 eggs
1 1/2 cups light cream (half and half)
Nutmeg

On floured surface, roll pastry into a 14-inch circle. Transfer to deep dish pan. Turn edges of dough under, trimming if needed, shaping so that edge is flush with rim of pan. Prick bottom and sides with a fork. Bake at 375° for 15 minutes, following directions on page 82 for baked pastry shell. Let cool about 20 minutes before filling.

Steam broccoli just until tender crisp. Season to taste with salt and lemon juice. Spread prepared pastry with mustard. Spoon broccoli evenly over the mustard and sprinkle top with the shredded cheese. Beat the eggs with the cream until thoroughly mixed.

Pour egg mixture over surface of the prepared quiche. Sprinkle with nutmeg. Bake at 375° for 35 to 40 minutes until center is just set. Cool on a rack for 10 minutes before cuting into wedges to serve.

QUICHE FOR TWO

Superstone Quiche For Two is a set of individual quiche dishes. Ready to be filled with a variety of ingredients, the shells are handy to have made ahead for quick and easy suppers or lunches. Six to eight individual quiche shells are needed to use in place of a regular deep dish pastry shell. The following recipes are proportioned for two servings.

To make the crust, prepare half the Classic Tart Pastry recipe, page 80, using 1 egg yolk in place of the whole egg. Refrigerate dough as directed. On lightly floured surface, roll dough into an oblong so that 2 circles, about 8 inches in diameter, can be cut. (I use a saucepan lid as a guide.) Line the quiche pans with the pastry, turning edges under and shaping to form an edge that is a little higher than the rim of the pan. Prick bottom with a fork in a few places. Bake in a 400° oven for 10 to 12 minutes until pastry just begins to brown. Remove quiche shells from oven, reduce oven temperature to 350°.

To make the filling, beat 1 egg with 1/2 cup light cream and 1/4 tsp. Dijon-style mustard or dry mustard.

To bake quiches, place in 350° oven for 15 to 20 minutes, until knife inserted in center comes out clean.

To serve, let quiche stand 5 minutes. Garnish with chopped fresh herbs and fresh vegetable relishes, such as zucchini slices, carrot curls, cherry tomato roses, or cooked broccoli or cauliflower flowerets.

For **Crab Quiche,** sprinkle bottom of prepared quiche shells with 1/4 cup parmesan cheese. Add 1/2 cup flaked cooked crabmeat (or cooked cut-up fresh or frozen shrimp) and 3/4 cup shredded Gruyere, Emmentaler, or Jarlsberg Swiss cheese. Add a dash of hot pepper sauce to filling. Divide filling between quiches. Bake.

For **Cheese Spinach Quiches,** cook 1/4 pound fresh spinach (or 1/4 of a 10-ounce pkg. frozen spinach, thawed); drain well. Spoon into quiche shells. Top with 3/4 cup shredded fontina, Swiss, or cheddar cheese. Divide filling between quiches. Bake.

For **Seafood Quiches,** saute 2 green onions (use part of tops) in 1 tbsp. butter until onions are limp. Combine onions with 1/2 cup leftover baked or poached fish. Spoon into prepared quiche shells. Top with 1/2 cup shredded mild Swiss or Monterrey Jack cheese. Divide filling between quiches. Sprinkle lightly with paprika. Bake.

For **French Onion Quiches,** saute 1 medium chopped onion in 2 tbsp. butter until soft. Spoon onion into prepared quiche shells. Top with 1/2 cup Swiss cheese. Divide filling between quiches. Sprinkle lightly with nutmeg.

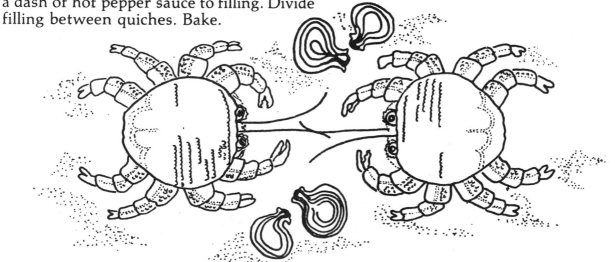

GARDEN VEGETABLE TART

A late summer supper that combines "what's in the garden," this tart should provide lots of creative ideas. Consider others flavors and colors when planning the layers and your variations can be as pretty, and delicious, as this one. Makes six to eight servings.

Parmesan Cornmeal Pastry, page 80

1/2 lb. Swiss chard, kale, or
   similar leafy vegetable
2 small zucchini, sliced (about 1/2 lbs.)
2 medium onions, chopped
2 tbsp. butter
1 cup thinly sliced ham, shredded
   (about 1/4 lb.)
1 cup fresh corn, cooked
   and drained
4 eggs
1 1/2 cups light cream (half and half)
Dash of cayenne pepper

On floured surface, roll pastry into a 14-inch circle. Transfer to deep dish pan. Turn edges of dough under, pinching to form a high fluted edge. Prick bottom and sides with a fork. Bake at 375° for 15 minutes, following directions on page 82 for baked pastry shells. Let cool about 20 minutes.

Thoroughly wash fresh chard; steam until wilted. Drain in colander. Steam zucchini just until tender crisp. Saute onions in butter until soft.

To assemble the quiche, spoon chard into prepared pastry. Add onions and ham in layers, then arrange a layer of zucchini and sprinkle with the corn. Beat eggs with the cream and cayenne pepper until thoroughly mixed.

Pour egg mixture over surface of prepared quiche. Bake at 375° for 40 to 45 minutes until center is just set. Cool on a rack for 10 minutes before cutting into wedges to serve.

STRAWBERRY RHUBARB TART

Makes eight servings.

Rich Tart Pastry, page 81

4 cups (1 quart) fresh ripe strawberries,
   hulled and halved
2 cups sliced rhubarb, cut in
   1-inch pieces
3/4 cup sugar
2 tbsp. flour
1 tbsp. grated orange peel

Streusel topping, page 83

On floured surface, roll pastry to a 14-inch circle. Transfer to deep dish pan. Turn edges of dough under, pinching to form high fluted edge.

Combine strawberries and rhubarb with sugar, flour and orange peel. Fill pastry shell with fruit mixture. Top fruit filling with streusel topping. Bake in a 425° oven for 45 to 50 minutes until juice in center of pie is bubbly.

GREEK EGGPLANT TART

Traditional moussaka ingredients flavor this meatless entree that is a hearty buffet favorite. Makes six to eight servings.

Classic Tart Pastry, page 80

1 medium eggplant (about 1 1/2—2 lbs.)
Salt
8—10 Italian plum tomatoes **or**
   2 large "meaty" tomatoes
2 medium onions, chopped
2 tbsp. butter
3—4 tbsp. olive oil
1/4 cup chopped fresh parsley
3—4 tbsp. freshly grated
   parmesan cheese

Cream Sauce:
4 tbsp. butter
1/4 cup all-purpose flour
2 cups milk
3 egg yolks
Salt and white pepper
Pinch of allspice or nutmeg
3—4 tbsp. freshly grated
   parmesan cheese

Peel and cut up eggplant into cubes; place in a colander. Sprinkle with salt and let drain for at least 1 hour. Peel, slice, and drain tomatoes. Roll out and partially bake the tart shell as directed on page 82.

In large skillet, saute onions in 2 tbsp. butter until soft. Remove from skillet and set aside. In the same skillet, heat 3 tbsp. olive oil, add the eggplant cubes, and cook until well browned; drain on paper towels.

Meanwhile, prepare cream sauce by melting butter in a heavy saucepan; add the flour. Cook for a minute or two without browning. Slowly add milk, whisking until mixture is smooth and thickened. Remove from heat and add egg yolks, blending well. Season to taste with salt, pepper and allspice.

To assemble the tart, spoon eggplant into the prepared tart shell. Add half the tomatoes, saving the best halves or slices for the top. Sprinkle with half the parsley. Add the onions, then add remaining tomatoes, arranging them in an attractive pattern. Sprinkle with remaining parsley. Pour in cream sauce, and sprinkle with cheese.

Bake in a 350° oven for 40 to 45 minutes until top is golden brown and filling is set. Let stand about 20 minutes before cutting into wedges.

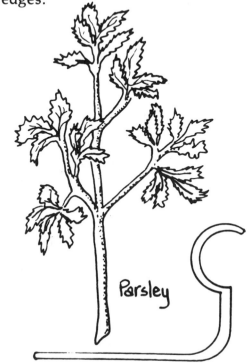

Parsley

CINNAMON PEAR TART

A classic open-faced tart made with pears or apples is a favorite late summer pie. Serve topped with whipped cream. Makes eight servings.

Rich Tart Pastry, page 81

1/2 cup brown sugar
2 tbsp. all-purpose flour
1 tbsp. grated orange peel
1 tsp. cinnamon
1/2 tsp. nutmeg
1/2 tsp. ginger

2 tbsp. orange juice
2 tbsp. melted butter
4 large fresh firm pears, peeled, cored and thinly sliced

Apricot Glaze, made with 1/2 cup apricot jam heated with 1 tbsp. water (optional)

On floured surface, roll pastry into a 14-inch circle. Transfer to deep dish pan. Turn edges of dough under, trimming if needed, and shape with fingers so that edge is flush with the rim of the pan.

Combine brown sugar, flour, orange peel, and spices, set aside. Arrange a layer of pears in pastry shell; sprinkle with half the brown sugar mixture. Arrange remaining pear slices in overlapping concentric circles atop the first layer; sprinkle with remaining brown sugar. Drizzle with orange juice and butter. Bake in a 375° oven for about 35 minutes, or until pear slices are soft and crust is golden. Let cool to room temperature. Glaze by spooning warm apricot mixture over pears.

PIZZAS
Yeast Crusts

The popularity of deep dish-style pizzas is spreading from Chicago and the midwest. These pizzas are characterized by cheese -- lots of it -- that is placed on the dough as the first layer of the pizza. The tomato sauce or, more typically chopped Italian plum tomato, is spooned on as the last layer. It's traditional pizza in reverse, and a hearty serving in one slice.

To make the dough, follow the Basic Pizza Crust recipe on page 33, then shape as described here.

TRADITIONAL CHICAGO-STYLE DEEP DISH PIZZA

Makes six to eight servings

Basic Pizza Crust, page 33

3/4 to 1 lb. mozzarella cheese, sliced

1 lb. fresh, peeled or 1 can (28 oz.) Italian plum tomatoes, chopped and well drained

2 tbsp. fresh oregano

1/2 cup freshly grated parmesan and/or romano cheese

Prepare pizza crust. Transfer the dough to deep dish pizza pan, shaping so that edge is flush with rim of the pan. Place mozzarella cheese slices over the bottom of the unbaked crust, layering as needed. Top cheese with your favorite filling ingredients. Add tomato and oregano; then sprinkle with parmesan cheese. Bake in a 450° oven for 25 to 30 minutes until crust is golden and filling is bubbly. Let set a few minutes before serving.

BACON, ONION, AND CHEESE PIZZA

Makes six to eight servings.

Basic Pizza Crust, page 33

1/2 lb. sliced bacon, cut in
    quarters
1 large onion, coarsely chopped
1/2—3/4 pound shredded mozzarella
    cheese
1 1/2 cups Fresh Tomato Sauce, page 34
1/2 cup pitted ripe olives, sliced or
    halved
1/4 cup freshly grated parmesan cheese

Prepare pizza crust. Transfer to deep dish pizza pan, shaping so that the edge is flush with the rim of the pan.

Fry bacon until crisp; let drain on paper towels. Reserve 2 tbsp. bacon drippings and saute onion until soft.

To assemble pizza, sprinkle about half the mozzarella cheese into the unbaked crust. Spoon onions over cheese and top with bacon. Spread tomato sauce over bacon. Sprinkle with olives and remaining mozzarella and parmesan cheese. Bake in a 450° oven for 25 to 30 minutes until crust is golden and filling is bubbly as directed. Let set a few minutes before serving.

"SOUTH OF THE BORDER" DEEP DISH PIZZA

Makes six to eight servings.

Basic Pizza Crust, page 33

3/4—1 lb. lean ground beef or
    pork sausage
1 small onion, chopped
1 clove garlic, minced
1/4 cup catsup
1—2 tbsp. chili powder
Dash of cayenne pepper
Jalapeno peppers
3/4—1 lb. shredded Monterrey Jack
    and/or colby cheese
1/2 cup Mexican salsa
    (tomato and chili sauce)

Prepare pizza crust. Transfer to deep dish pizza pan, shaping so that the edge is flush with the rim of the pan.

Brown ground beef with onion and garlic in large skillet; drain. Add catsup, chili powder, and cayenne pepper; simmer about 5 minutes.

Sprinkle about two-thirds of the cheese into the unbaked crust. Add Jalapeno peppers to suit your taste. Spoon in the ground beef mixture and top with the salsa. Sprinkle with remaining cheese. Bake in a 450° oven for 25 to 30 minutes until crust is golden and filling is bubbly. Let set a few minutes before serving.

For **Mexican Bean and Cheese Pizza**, omit ground beef and ground beef seasonings. Use 1 can (16 oz.) refried beans instead. Adjust seasoning accordingly.

CHILI BEAN TAMALE PIE

Makes six to eight servings.

1 1/2 cups stone-ground yellow cornmeal
1 1/2 cups water
1 tsp. salt
2 cups boiling water
2 tbsp. butter or margarine

2 medium onions, chopped
1 green pepper, chopped
1 stalk celery, chopped
2 cloves garlic, minced
3 tbsp. olive oil,
   butter, or margarine

2 cups (16 oz. can) red kidney
   beans, drained
1 1/2 cups (12 oz. can) tomatoes with
   green chilies, partly drained
1 can (6 oz.) tomato paste
Salt, cayenne or black pepper
1/2 cup sliced green olives
1 1/2—2 cups shredded colby, cheddar
   or Monterrey Jack cheese

In medium saucepan, stir together cornmeal, 1 1/2 cups water, and salt. Stirring constantly. Gradually pour in 2 cups boiling water and bring mixture to boiling, stirring constantly. Partially cover pan and cook over low heat for 7 to 10 minutes, stirring often. Stir in butter. Set aside while preparing filling.

In large skillet over medium heat, saute onion, green pepper, celery, and garlic in olive oil until vegetables are limp. Stir in beans, tomatoes, and tomato paste. Simmer about 10 minutes until sauce is thickened. Taste, season with salt, cayenne or black pepper, as desired.

Sprinkle bottom of deep dish pan with dry cornmeal. Spread about two-thirds of the cornmeal mixture over the bottom and up the sides of the pan to form a shell. Spoon bean mixture into the cornmeal shell. Sprinkle with olives. Spoon remaining cornmeal mixture over top in mounds in a circular pattern. Bake, covered loosely with a piece of foil, at 400° for 30 minutes. Uncover, sprinkle with cheese, and continue baking an additional 10 to 15 minutes, until cheese melts and pie is thoroughly heated.

TAMALE DEEP DISH PIE

A hearty meal in one dish, tamale pies are derived from Mexican tamales, a cornmeal mixture that is wrapped in corn husks and steamed. Tamale Deep Dish Pie is a traditional meat version, while Chili Bean Tamale Pie is meatless. The combination of cornmeal, red kidney beans, and cheese make this dish a complete, and very economical, protein source. Makes six to eight servings.

1 1/2 cups stone-ground yellow cornmeal
1 1/2 cups water
1 tsp. salt
2 cups boiling water
2 tbsp. butter, margarine, or lard

3/4—1 lb. lean ground beef or
    pork sausage
1 large onion, chopped
1/2 large green pepper, chopped
1 tbsp. chili seasoning or powder
1/2 tbsp. ground cumin
1 clove garlic, minced
3 "meaty" tomatoes, peeled, seeded
    and chopped
1 can (12 oz.) whole kernel corn or
    1 1/2 cups fresh corn,
    cut from the cob
Salt and pepper
1/2 cup pitted ripe olives, sliced
1 cup (4 oz.) shredded Monterrey
    Jack cheese

In medium saucepan, stir together cornmeal, 1 1/2 cups water and salt. Gradually pour in 2 cups boiling water, stirring contantly. Bring mixture to a boil. Partially cover pan and cook over low heat for 7 to 10 minutes, stirring often. Stir in butter. Set aside while preparing filling.

In large skillet over medium heat, brown ground beef with onion, green pepper, chili seasoning, cumin, and garlic. Stir in tomatoes and corn. Simmer about 10 minutes until most of the liquid has evaporated. Taste; season with salt and pepper.

Sprinkle bottom of deep dish pan with dry cornmeal. Spread about two-thirds of the cornmeal mixture over the bottom and up the sides of the pan to form a shell. Spoon meat mixture into the cornmeal shell. Sprinkle with olives. Spoon remaining cornmeal mixture over top in mounds in a circular pattern. Bake, covered loosely with a piece of foil, at 400° for 30 minutes. Uncover, sprinkle with cheese, and continue baking an additional 10 to 15 minutes until cheese melts and pie is thoroughly heated.

INDEX

A

Anadama Bread 24
Applesauce Nut Cake 61
Apricot Oatmeal Bread 56

B

Bacon, Onion and Cheese Pizza 94
Baking Crocks 51
   Sugar Top Loaves 21
   Walnut Fruit Bread 61
   Whole Grain Herb Bread 53
   Whole Grain Sesame Bread 53
Banana Poundcake 60
Banneton, shaping loaf 19
Basic Pizza Crust 33
Beef and Cheese Biscuit Wedges 38
Beer Marinated Pot Roast 72
Biscuits:
   Beef and Cheese Biscuit Wedges 38
   Wholewheat Currant Scones 38
Brandy Hardsauce· 58
Bread Sticks or Pretzels 25
Bread Sticks, Salty Italian 25
Breads, baking "undercover" 66
Breads, baking with yeast 13
Breads, ingredients to make 14
Breads, steps in making batter yeast .. 51
Breads, steps in making yeast 16
Brown Butter Icing 58
Brunch Favorites:
   Apricot Oatmeal Bread 56
   Easy Norwegian Julekage 55
   Pecan Streusel Coffeecake 83
   Quiche Lorraine 86
   Raisin-Nut Bread 21
   Russian Easter Bread 57
   Scandinavian Cardamon Wreath 27
   Swedish Cardamon Braid 27
   Swiss Cheese Pie 87

Butter Rum Icing 58
Buttermilk Potato Bread 23

C

Cake glazes and sauces 58
Cakes:
   Applesauce Nut Cake 61
   Banana Poundcake 60
   Naturally Delicious Fruit Cake 59
   Pineapple Carrot Cake 62
Carioca Chocolate Bread 60
Challah 28
Cheddar Broccoli Quiche 88
Cheese and Spinach Quiches, for Two .. 89
Cheese Spread, Savory 58
Cheesy Beer Bread 54
Chili Bean Tamale Pie 95
Chocolate Chip Pecan Pie 85
Chocolate Pecan Pie 85
Cinnamon Pear Tart 92
Cinnamon-Raisin Bread 23
Classic Tart Pastry 80
Cookies:
   Double Peanut Blossoms 40
   Oatmeal Peanut Butter Cookies 40
   Salted Peanut Cookies 41
   Spicy Ginger Cookies 39
   Sunny Carrot Cookies 41
   Whole Wheat Chocolate Chip Cookies 42
Corn Syrup Glaze 58
Crab Quiches, for Two 89
Cracked Wheat Sourdough Bread 69
Creamy Peach Deep Dish Pie 84
Crusty Braided Loaves 21
Crusty Country Loaf 67
Crusty Country Rolls 24

INDEX

D

Deep Dish Pizza/Pie Baker 79
Whole Wheat Pastry 80
Dill Cheese Bread 54
Double Cheese Bread Twists 48
Double Peanut Blossoms 40
Dutch Cheese Apple Pie 86

E

Easy Norwegian Julekage 55
Egg washes and glazes for yeast breads 20
English Muffin Bread 52

F

Favorite Pecan Pie 85
Fillets of Sole with Mushroom Stuffing 77
Fish:
    Fillets of Sole with Mushroom Stuffing 77
    Halibut Steaks with Mushrooms and Shrimp 76
Flaky "Never Fail" Pastry 81
French Bread Baker 45
French Onion Quiches, for Two 89
Fresh Tomato Sauce for Pizza 34

G

Garden Vegetable Tart 90
Glazed Corned Beef with Carrots and Prunes . 72
Golden Butter Sauce 59
Graham Health Bread 22
Greek Eggplant Tart 91

H

Halibut Steaks with Mushrooms and Shrimp .. 76
Herb-Filled Sour Cream Loaves 49
Herbed Lamb Shank Dinner 73
Home-Style Honey Wheat Bread 21
Honey Egg Braid 28

I

Irish Oatmeal Bread, Sourdough 69
Italian Sesame Loaves 46

L

La Cloche 65
La Cloche Roasted Turkey Breast 76
Large Vienna Crescent 25

M

Meat Pastries:
    Pick-Me-Up Ham and Cheese Turnovers 37
    Pick-Me-Up Krautburgers 36
Meats:
    Beer Marinated Pot Roast 72
    Glazed Corned Beef with Carrots and Prunes 72
    Herbed Lamb Shank Dinner 73
    New England Style Corned Beef 73
    Pork Chops with Sweet Potatoes and Apples 74
    Wine Marinated Pot Roast 71
Mexican Bean and Cheese Pizza 94

N

Naturally Delicious Fruit Cake 59
New England Style Corned Beef 73

O

Oatmeal Peanut Butter Cookies 40
Onion Rolls 25
Orange Baked Chicken 75

P

Parmesan-Cornmeal Pastry 80
Pastry:
    Classic Tart Pastry 80
    Cheese Pastry 86
    Flaky "Never Fail" Pastry 81
    Parmesan-Cornmeal Pastry 80
    Rich Tart Pastry 81
    Sour Cream Tart Pastry 81
    Steps in making pie crusts and pastry shells . 82
    Using food processor for pastry 83
    Whole Wheat Pastry 80
Pear Mince Pie 84
Pecan Streusel Coffeecake 83
Pepperoni, Ham and Mushroom Pizza 35

INDEX

Pick-Me-Up Ham and Cheese Turnovers 37
Pick-Me-Up Krautburgers 36
Pick-Me-Up Sandwich Buns 36
Pies and Tarts, Dessert:
  Cinnamon Pear Tart 83
  Chocolate Chip Pecan Pie 85
  Chocolate Pecan Pie 85
  Creamy Peach Deep Dish Pie 84
  Dutch Cheese Apple Pie 87
  Favorite Pecan Pie 85
  Pear Mince Pie 86
  Strawberry Rhubarb Tart 84
  Streusel-Topped Melba Pie 85
  Streusel-Topped Peach Blueberry Pie 85
Pies and Tarts, Main Dish:
  Cheddar Broccoli Quiche 88
  Cheese and Spinach Quiches, for Two 89
  Crab Quiches, for Two 89
  French Onion Quiches, for Two 89
  Garden Vegetable Tart 90
  Greek Eggplant Tart 91
  Quiche for Two:
    Cheese and Spinach Quiches 89
    Crab Quiches 89
    French Onion Quiches 89
    Seafood Quiches 89
  Quiche Lorraine 86
  Savory Onion Quiche 87
  Savory Onion-Tomato Quiche 87
  Seafood Quiches, for Two 89
  Swiss Cheese Pie 87
Pineapple Carrot Cake 62
Pizza:
  Baking on Superstone® 13
  Bacon, Onion and Cheese Pizza 94
  Basic Pizza Crust 33
  Fresh Tomato Sauce for Pizza 34
  Mexican Bean and Cheese Pizza 94
  Pepperoni, Ham and Mushroom Pizza 35

  Salami on Rye Pizza 35
  "South of the Border" Deep Dish Pizza 94
  Traditional Cheese and Tomato Pizza 34
  Traditional Chicago-Style Deep Dish Pizza .. 93
Pork Chops with Sweet Potatoes and Apples ... 74
Pot roasting "undercover" 70
Poultry:
  La Cloche Roasted Turkey Breast 76
  Orange Baked Chicken 75
Pretzels, Bread Sticks or 25
Pretzels, Soft 25
Pueblo Indian Bread 68
Pumpkin Topknot Loaf 26

Q

Quiche for Two 88
Quiche Lorraine 86
Quick Breads:
  Carioca Chocolate Bread 60
  Walnut Fruit Bread 61

R

Raisin-Nut Bread 21
Rich Tart Pastry 81
Roasting meats "undercover" 70
Roasting poultry "undercover" 74
Russian Easter Bread 57
Rye Flour:
  Pick-Me-Up Sandwich Buns 36
  Salami on Rye Pizza 35
  Sourdough Onion Rye Bread 32
  Sourdough Rye Bread 32
  Two-Tone Rye Party Bread 47

S

Salami on Rye Pizza 35
Salted Peanut Cookies 41
Salty Italian Bread Sticks 25
Savory Cheese Spread 58
Savory Onion Quiche 87
Savory Onion-Tomato Quiche 87

INDEX

Scandinavian Cardamon Wreath 27
Seafood Quiches, for Two 89
Seven-Grain Whole Wheat Bread 22
Shaping Bread:
    Braided loaves 20
    Bread sticks 20
    English bloomer 20
    Pretzels 20
    Twist loaves 20
    Vienna loaf 20
Simple French Bread 46
Soft Pretzels 25
Sour Cream Herb Twists 25
Sour Cream Tart Pastry 81
Sourdough Breads:
    Cracked Wheat Sourdough Bread 69
    Sourdough French Bread 31
    Sourdough Irish Oatmeal Bread 69
    Sourdough Onion Rye Bread 32
    Sourdough Rye Bread 32
    Sourdough Starter 30
    Sourdough Started Batter 30
"South of the Border" Deep Dish Pizza 94
Spicy Ginger Cookies 39
Strawberry Rhubarb Tart 90
Streusel Apple Cake 83
Streusel Peach Cake 83
Streusel Plum Cake 83
Streusel-Topped Melba Pie 85
Streusel-Topped Peach Blueberry Pie 85
Streusel Topping 83
Sugar Top Loaves 21
Sunny Carrot Cookies 41
Superstone® Baking Stone and
    Superstone® Baking Tiles 13
Swedish Cardamon Braid 27
Swiss Cheese Pie 87

T

Tamale Deep Dish Pie 96
Tomato Sauce, Fresh, for Pizza 34

Traditional Cheese and Tomato Pizza 34
Traditional Chicago-Style Deep Dish Pizza 93
Two-Tone Rye Party Bread 47

V

Vienna Rolls 25

W

Walnut Fruit Bread 61
Whole Grain Country Loaves 67
Whole Grain Herb Bread 53
Whole Grain Sesame Bread 53
Whole Wheat Chocolate Chip Cookies 42
Whole Wheat Currant Scones 38
Whole Wheat Flour:
    Anadama Bread 24
    Bread Sticks or Pretzels 25
    Cinnamon-Raisin Bread 23
    Crusty Braided Loaves 21
    Graham Health Bread 22
    Home-Style Honey Wheat Bread 21
    Raisin-Nut Bread 21
    Seven-Grain Whole Wheat Bread 22
    Spicy Ginger Cookies 39
    Traditional Cheese and Tomato Pizza 34
    Whole Grain Country Loaves 67
    Whole Grain Herb Bread 53
    Whole Grain Sesame Bread 53
    Whole Wheat Chocolate Chip Cookies 42
    Whole Wheat Currant Scones 38
    Whole Wheat Pastry 80
Wine Marinated Pot Roast 71

Y

Yeast bread baking 13
Yeast bread, baking "undercover" 66
Yeast bread, ingredients in 14
Yeast bread, shaping loaves 19
Yeast breads, batter 52
Yeast crusts 93